The Paralegal's Desk Reference

Steve Albrecht

foreword by **John W. Witt**
City Attorney, San Diego, California

PRENTICE HALL

New York • London • Toronto • Sydney • Tokyo • Singapore

Prentice Hall General Reference
15 Columbus Circle
New York, NY 10023

An Arco Book

Arco, Prentice Hall, and colophons are
registered trademarks of Simon & Schuster, Inc.

Library of Congress Cataloging-in-Publication Data

The paralegal's desk reference / Steve Albrecht; foreword by John W. Witt
    p. cm.
  ISBN 0-671-84715-5
  1. Legal assistants--United States--Handbooks, manuals, etc.
I. Title.
KF320.L4A33   1993   92-44325
340'.023'73—dc20   CIP

Manufactured in the United States of America

1 2 3 4 5 6 7 8 9 10

First Edition

contents

acknowledgments

*L*ong ago, during a high school English class, the subject of college marching bands somehow came up. My English teacher, a wry if somewhat cynical man, offered the opinion that during any football game half-time period there are only four people who truly care if a marching band is even on the field: the person on the field playing the instrument and marching around; his or her proud parents seated in the stands; and his or her girlfriend or boyfriend.

While this narrow view certainly puts a damper on the concept of "school spirit," it does bring up an interesting parallel for book authors. Who, besides the people mentioned, really cares about the names on the always-popular "Acknowledgments" page? Only the people mentioned.

However, since few authors can honestly admit that their work did not involve some help and support from friends, peers, and colleagues, so it would be unfair for me to continue without thanking the following attorneys: Linda Godinez, Esq. from Rose, Klein, and Marias; Ernest Georggin and Michael Shann, Esqs., and staff; Vaughan de Kirby, Esq., and staff; and the following paralegal pros: Gina Peña and Monica Reitano.

Many thanks to my editor, Eve Steinberg, for her unflagging patience and marked ability to see diamonds amid the coal. Thanks also to my father, Karl, a bestselling author who has been through the book "birthing" process many times. And finally, thanks to my wife, Leslie, who understands that I'm working even when I'm sleeping on the couch in my office.

about the author

Steve Albrecht is an instructor for Albrecht Training & Development, a San Diego–based company specializing in business writing, added-value negotiating, service management, and law enforcement training seminars. He has a B.A. degree in English from the University of San Diego and is nationally known for his written work on law enforcement issues.

Mr. Albrecht has been with the San Diego Police Department since 1984, both as a regular officer and now as a reserve officer. A member of the American Society of Law Enforcement Trainers and the American Society of Training and Development, he contributes articles and columns to police publications across the country.

He is the author of *Streetwork: The Way To Police Officer Safety and Survival*, and he co-wrote *Contact and Cover: Two-Officer Suspect Control* with John Morrison. He also co-authored *The Creative Corporation* and *Added Value Negotiating* with his father, Karl Albrecht, and has written several hundred mass-market, business, and criminal justice articles along with a number of audiotape training programs.

In 1988, while working for an accident investigation firm that handled cases for 35 plaintiff and defense attorneys, Mr. Albrecht designed and taught a full-day seminar for paralegals that became the basis for this book.

foreword

*P*aralegals are not newly arrived on the scene, but extensive development of the paralegal profession has occurred over a period which roughly coincides with my career at the Bar. From their limited beginnings in the private sector, professional paralegals have become a highly visible and well-appreciated presence in government law offices as well.

Law office managers in both the public and the private sector are discovering the expanded scope of work that is possible with use of a competent paralegal program. Individual lawyers are also learning to apply paralegal services to their existing workloads and thereby to increase effective use of their own time.

Steve Albrecht has compiled a useful paralegal reference book. It will be of enormous value not only to paralegals but also to the attorneys who employ and manage them. Lawyers would be well advised to study Mr. Albrecht's book in order to better understand their own roles with respect to paralegals. Those who do not now employ paralegals should be able to ascertain whether paralegals would make professional and economic sense in their practices. Those who already utilize paralegal services can find innovative ways to improve their use.

Of course, the book is principally designed for the use of paralegals themselves. No matter how experienced and talented a paralegal may be, he or she can find in it new and useful information with which to improve performance. As Mr. Albrecht points out, skilled paralegals carry significant portions of the workload in the law firms that employ them. His book will help them to help themselves and their employers by increasing their professional efficiency.

In today's government law office, efficient use of paralegal skills is becoming vital as already sparse budgets become tighter. The San Diego City Attorney's office makes good use of paralegals, particularly in our criminal and civil litigation divisions. In an era when budget restrictions mean we cannot replace employees who leave city service, it is as important, if not more important, to retain paralegals as it is to retain attorneys. To the extent that we can maximize their value to us through implementation of the techniques offered in this book, we do ourselves and the public a great service.

I intend to reexamine our utilization of paralegals in light of Mr. Albrecht's suggestions. It seems likely that I will find valuable ways to increase the effectiveness of our professional operations in areas other than those in which our paralegals perform now. Hopefully, I will find ways to benefit my staff, the city government, and the public by providing "more bang for the buck" in expanded paralegal services.

John W. Witt, City Attorney
San Diego, California

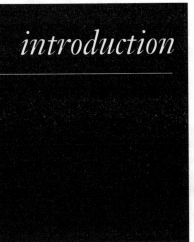

introduction

The paralegal profession can be tremendously challenging, time-intensive, and rewarding. But above all else, it involves a great deal of hard work. If you've been involved with the legal profession in any capacity for any length of time, I'm sure you'll agree that paralegals and legal assistants do the bulk of the work around most attorneys' offices. This may sound like a bold statement, but it's most certainly true.

It's not my aim to downplay the "lawyering" skills of our attorneys, nor do I want to sound like the speaker for the paralegal profession. But I have worked in and around enough law offices to recognize certain divisions of labor.

Attorneys who work in small, midsize, or large firms must have the knowledge, training, educational background, and professional expertise to attract clients and settle their cases, but the day-to-day, "grind-it-out" paperwork and client management are usually handled by the paralegal staff.

For example, it should come as no surprise that many successful personal injury attorneys follow a "formula" that applies to nearly all clients. A number of the largest and most prosperous law firms specializing in personal injury cases spend an enormous amount of money on radio and television advertising spots, all designed to generate client interest and increase word-of-mouth referrals. Under the right economic and creative circumstances, these targeted ad campaigns can bring in dozens of new clients every week. And from the first moment the client enters the office until the time when the case settles, he or she is guided down a well-paved "road" by the attorneys and their paralegal support staff.

Typical car-accident personal injury law offices offer "one-stop" service, meaning that they will handle everything, from the client's medical bills and auto repairs to the rental car payments, insurance company negotiations, demand letters, and settlement packages. Except for providing the necessary information and completing a prescribed medical treatment program, the client has few worries.

The attorneys and their paralegals in these large, efficient personal injury firms have handled hundreds of similar cases and can take the client from start to finish just by following the same procedures and plugging in the same formulas. Preparing forms, establishing procedures, and creating prepared letters in advance leaves very little to chance or staff haphazardness. By following these time-tested procedures and using so-called boilerplate documents to settle the case, paralegals can handle most of the work right up to the moment when the attorneys step in to finalize everything to the satisfaction of both sides.

While I'm certainly not suggesting that attorneys in these firms do nothing but "make rain" (gather new clients) and take long lunches, I have seen a number of skilled paralegals carry the bulk of the load for an entire law firm. These dedicated paralegals have taken clients through the entire legal process, updating them as necessary, even providing sympathy and support during highly emotional depositions, hearings, or court cases. In short, the best paralegals do more than their fair share of the work and deserve credit when it's due.

In 1988, I taught a full-day seminar for new paralegals. I originally intended to teach them how to work as pseudoinvestigators by explaining the process that surrounds most personal injury, worker's compensation, or criminal defense cases. The more I taught the course, the more I learned about paralegals: their goals, apprehensions, anxieties, and work responsibilities. I began to direct my training efforts towards the kinds of "inside" information that they could use the most.

My work as an accident investigator helped me to see what was important to attorneys and what they expected from their paralegal and legal assistant staffs in turn. I tried to take my observations from the real world of the law office and fit them into the needs of the new paralegal.

So if you're new to the paralegal profession, here's an important piece of advice to consider as you go through this book: read, reread, and reread again. Mark the pages with bookmarks, sticky notes, or paperclips; dogear the corners for future reference; use a yellow marking pen on the more significant sections; and generally treat this book as your own personal desk reference. The time you save by following the procedures and techniques I suggest is not just your own; it belongs to your boss, your clients, and the firm you work for.

This book will not turn you into an attorney or a private investigator. Rather, it will teach you to use already existing resources to gather information critical to the success of your cases.

If you've been in the paralegal profession for a while, you may be quite familiar with some of the information I discuss. Some of the ideas and concepts may work well for you and others may not. Only your experience can tell you what to do. Rest assured that this book will not suggest you do anything unethical, or worse, illegal. Feel free to choose what you can use. Your career development begins from your first day on the job and never ends.

Additionally, if you're an experienced paralegal, the best way to enhance your sense of professionalism is to help less-experienced paralegals to catch on. You should know by now that the legal field can be extremely stressful, time-pressured, and unnerving. Faced with a large caseload, demanding attorneys, and rattled clients, the job can seem twice as difficult to a new paralegal.

If you can offer additional shortcuts, time-savers, and helpful advice about office management (and office politics), case-handling and case-management shortcuts, client relations, and attorney-paralegal protocol to the newer members on your staff, please do so.

To quote the appropriate Latin phrase, *Qui docet, discet,* which means, "They who teach, learn."

I hope this book will reach paralegals at all levels of job experience and training. Whether it's used as a guidebook for people new to the profession or as a refresher for senior paralegals, I want the book to educate everyone who reads it.

As a seminar leader who teaches one- and two-day courses, I always have great expectations that my students will leave my classroom filled with everything I've taught and ready to put the information to use. Experience tells me that if the class participants can really grasp four or five key concepts, then I've done my job. Books offer no exception to that rule.

Read the text with your own law office in mind. Take some of the key concepts and really study them. You'll know what you can use immediately, and you'll apply it to your own needs and your short- and long-term goals. Remember that some of the material may not apply to you immediately, but no one can say you won't change firms, change legal specialties, or go in a completely new direction somewhere down the road.

Studies tell us that the era of the so-called 10-year employee is on the downswing. One, three, or five years from now, you may have already gone from a real estate law firm to a personal injury office to a criminal defense specialist. The beauty of the paralegal profession is its inherent flexibility. If you know a little bit about a lot of diverse legal subjects, you're clearly a more valuable commodity to a law firm looking to expand its paralegal force.

Be flexible and open-minded as you study this book. Take what you can use now, file the rest away in your head, and refer to it again as you grow and develop in your career. Keep your *Paralegal's Desk Reference* handy at your desk so you'll know how to go about finding the information you need.

one

GATHERING INFORMATION: What to Do When the File Hits Your Desk

"I keep six honest serving men/They taught me all I knew:/Their names are What and Why and When/And How and Where and Who."— Rudyard Kipling

*I*t's good news–bad news time. The good news is that the law firm you work for has a whole roomful of new clients, and business couldn't be better. The bad news is that the law firm you work for has a whole roomful of clients, and business couldn't be better.

More work for the attorneys in your firm certainly means more work for you. It's easy to get bogged down as the case files pile up on your desk. Worse yet, if two or three cases involve specific challenges that take you away from the more standard cases, you can find yourself giving short shrift to your clients. This can only lead to missed deadlines, angry phone calls from clients to your boss, and a feeling that you're swamped with work and up against the wall.

If this scenario fits you and the office where you work, you're not alone. The legal industry in the U.S. is booming. More and more lawyers are graduating from law school, passing their state bar exams, and entering the workforce than ever before. Along with this continuing rise in the number of attorneys comes another significant rise from within the paralegal profession. As attorneys start their own practices, become associates at large and midsize law firms, or join the government or major companies as corporate counsel, they require an increase in the staff support offered by paralegals.

Since the legal profession is on the upswing, it makes sense that the paralegal profession is too. But as you've probably already noticed, new clients, larger dollar-amount cases, and the growing number of court suits mean more work for everyone involved. And if you've worked as a paralegal for even a short time, you already know how hard the work can be. So how do you fit 10 hours of work into an eight-hour day? Three words: Organize, organize, organize.

The secret to successful case management, client management, time management, and (just as important) attorney management is to organize yourself and your office before the firestorm of clients, cases, and attorneys hits. The best way to establish a marching plan for each case is to create an ideal office environment.

Easy to say and hard to do? Not if you concentrate on a few important organizational basics.

Keeping Track

If you work for a midsize to large law firm, most of the organizational problems you'll face can be easily solved by the case management systems already in place. Someone has probably come before you and created filing systems, copying procedures, and similar tracking methods to run the office in a seemingly smooth manner.

If this is the case where you work, by all means learn these systems as rapidly as you can and stick to them. There are probably dozens of reasons why this case management system is in place to begin with: maximum attorney convenience, maximum paralegal convenience, space and office size limitations, attorney and staff limitations, and most importantly, because everyone recalls case management problems in the past.

Few things will turn an attorney's hair gray faster than a missing file and the resulting client anger it can cause. In most cases, the file "miraculously" appears after a few frantic hours of searching, and then all's well that ends well. However, if this becomes a common occurrence in the office, serious problems can arise.

I've read shocking accounts of lawyer malpractice in various attorney magazines. A common theme is the reckless mismanagement of client records. In some cases, this flagrant malfeasance has led to the dismissal of clients' multimillion-dollar lawsuits. In other cases lucrative contracts have fallen through; in still others massive probate problems have been created. Professional relationships are often ruined when successor attorneys try to salvage a lost client from a disorganized lawyer or law firm.

All horror stories aside, if your office uses a file and case management system that proves useful, stay with it. Some systems run via computer software programs specifically created for law practice management. Other paper-based tracking systems are so streamlined that even an earthquake couldn't disrupt them. Whatever system your office currently uses—computerized client files, standard paper files, or whatever—learn it well and add value by constantly searching for ways to improve it.

Some progressive law firms encourage their employees, attorneys, paralegals, and support staff alike, to come up with new and better ways to track cases, handle clients, and run the office more efficiently. Keep alert to contributions you might make with respect to record-keeping systems.

If you work for a firm with an efficient system already in place, you are in luck. But what if you work for a young, small firm, for a new single practitioner, or for an attorney who has broken away from an established firm to start a private practice with good legal skills but no familiarity with office infrastructures?

What do you do if you're called upon to create and maintain a case management and file-tracking system for you and other support staff to follow? Don't despair. Help is always available, and the solutions are relatively easy to implement. Putting case management plans into effect requires three important tools: some money, some time, and some rules. Notice the key word in this last sentence is "some." Good small-practice management, while certainly not free, does not require a huge outlay of money to introduce.

In most small-practice offices (and in larger firms wishing to change their current procedures) your choices come down to two options: a computerized system with minimum paper backup or a paper system alone. Here, the phrase "paper system" refers to the use of file folders to keep track of all correspondence, depositions, contracts, etc.

The choice depends largely on the volume of the practice and the skills, needs, and requirements of the attorneys and their support staff. Is the practice based on a high-volume, high-turnover personal injury clientele? Or is it more methodical and sedate, preferring to concentrate its efforts on the needs of a few high-dollar clients? Are the paralegal and associated support staffs geared toward paper systems, or do they have enough computer knowledge to make extensive training and retraining unnecessary?

Computer-Based Practice
Management

As we prepare to speed through the 1990s en route to the year 2000, it's plain to see that the computer is here to stay. By now, even the worst technophobe among us has come to the conclusion that he or she must have at least a budding familiarity with the green-glowing box of microchips known as the personal computer (PC). If you're not computer-literate, a basic course will be a real asset to your career. Ideally, you want the flexibility to operate as an effective paralegal in any office with any filing system and the eventual expertise to introduce improvements.

Some law firms have made the inevitable switch to computerized systems with hardly a sigh. Others have had to drag their employees kicking and screaming into the future.

A computer-based system offers several unique advantages over a paper-file system for a firm of any size. Consider the following reasons to move into the Information Age:

Speed: You can get instant updates on the status of a case at the touch of a button. Most software programs allow you to keep track of individual files by entering the client's last name or file record

4

number. In seconds, the entire electronic file appears, giving dates, deadlines, and court appearance and deposition information. With this system in place, you can get an entire case history right on the screen.

Accuracy: While it's not true that computers never make mistakes, the structure of most legal and practice management software programs won't allow you to enter improper data or make many mistakes. Storing client information on computers forces you to follow careful data entry procedures. It's a powerful asset when combined with good computer-use habits such as finishing each entry task in order, updating the cases when necessary, and protecting the computer from harm just as if it were a living member of the office staff.

Safety: With the prudent use of all-important backup floppy disks, hard disk drive backup systems, and careful handling of the software and hardware, the computer can work for years and years without failure. Some law offices lock their computerized client files (the backup disks or tapes themselves) into a sturdy safe at the end of each business day. This protects the client files—truly the lifeblood of any law firm—from fire, water damage, or theft.

Confidentiality: Paper files left in standard filing cabinets don't offer much security from theft or sabotage, nor do they keep prying eyes away. Some legal software programs offer encryption protection, meaning that if you don't enter the proper password, employee ID number, or literally the correct key for the lockable keyhole, you don't get in. This protects the files from accidental or deliberate erasure and from any other electronic eavesdropping that might take place.

With such a wide range of computer software programs designed specifically for the needs of a law practice, it just makes good sense to take advantage of the power offered by a personal computer.

Some more sophisticated software programs allow you to create so-called boilerplate forms for use with attorneys and clients. Using form-creation software, you can set up an infinite number of in-house forms, contracts, waivers, leases, agreements, medical and information releases, wills, trusts, etc., that relate specifically to your firm and the type of law it practices.

While the price of specific law firm and practice management software programs can run from $100 floppy disks to $25,000 customized network systems that link dozens of computers together, the price of a high-quality PC ranges from a low end of about $500 to a high end of $5,000 or more. Clearly, the choice of which machine to buy and which system to implement is up to the attorneys running the office, the office manager, or a similar person with access to the company purse strings. A word to the wise, however, is that it's always best to buy slightly more expensive equipment that may offer more "bells and whistles" than you think you might need right now. It's risky to skimp on the computer hardware and software products used to keep track of your valuable clients. Buy reliable computer equipment and software now and save an inevitable headache later.

Since I've already discussed the spend-some-money concept in detail, let's turn to the set-aside-some-time factor.

The Systems in Action

Few paralegals were born with the knowledge required to run a bustling law office (although some may give that impression). New paralegals, associated support staff, and even the attorneys will need to familiarize themselves with any new office management or case handling systems. If you're in charge of training the entire office to use some new procedures, keep this in mind and take your patience pills as necessary.

Engineers write computer programs. And those same engineers often write the computer software manuals. If you don't speak "engineer," your computer familiarization process could take quite a while, both for you and your office-mates. If you're in charge of the training, allow your colleagues to learn at their own paces. Answer their questions, provide some helpful advice and examples to follow, and give them some selected positive reinforcement to keep up morale. Above all, allow more than enough time to get everyone in the office comfortable and up to speed with any new computer systems.

With money and time out of the way, our focus shifts to rules. A society without rules is a society in chaos. Similarly, an office without its own hard and fast rules is an office in chaos. Shoddy work habits, poor organizational methods, and outdated or poorly designed systems cause missing or incomplete files to become the norm rather than the exception. In a busy law practice, chaos is totally unacceptable.

In a computerized office, you need to establish a set of rules about who has access to the software files and when and how the files are updated, printed, purged, etc. The "too many cooks spoil the broth" theory applies here. If many people can get into the computer files and add, change, or delete things willy-nilly, the potential for disaster looms large. If it's your job to update the client files, do it alone. Don't allow other people to gum up the process.

If it falls on you to choose a fellow staffer to be the designated "data entry/computer person," use good judgement and select the one with the most computer experience, not just the most legal knowledge. With a computer-literate staffer in place, you'll save training time, prevent lost data problems, and preserve your peace of mind.

If your office runs on a paper system, strictly using client file folders to keep track of each case, you'll need to tighten the rules and procedures even more than with the computer method.

Here, checklists make the most sense, and many law offices use them in one form or another. The reasoning and the history behind these checklists is clear: If every time you go into a specific file you document your work, anyone else who comes along and reviews that file (an attorney, another paralegal, an investigator, etc.) will know what has been done, when it was done, and equally important for purposes of follow-up, by whom it was done.

Imagine picking up a thick case file and looking into it, only to see no record of activity for the last six months. Has the statute expired? Is the client finished treatment with the doctor? Did escrow close correctly on the real estate deal? Is it ready for trial? Has the case been given a court date? Has the other side made an offer? Have we made a counter-offer? What is the name of the insurance adjuster, opposing counsel, or outside litigator? Has the case settled, and have we or the client received payment? The possible questions are nearly endless, and the resulting number of "Who knows?" answers is even worse.

As I said before, if you work in an office with an established paper file system in place, stick with it and follow it correctly. The headaches (and the job) you save more than make up for a bit of extra time or seeming inconvenience on your part.

Some firms go so far as to post the "File Handling Rules" in various key places around the office, such as in the copy room, the employee break room, and in each work area.

Here's a sample list of 10 proven paper system rules that can apply in nearly every office:

1. *Label all files the same way*—by the client's typewritten last name; by the company name; or by a file number that corresponds to the date the case was opened, the type of case, or any other convenient tracking method.

2. *Always attach the standard office file checklist to the inside left facing page of the file folder.*

3. *Always sign the individual file cabinet log with the name of the file you removed, the date, and your name or initials.* (Failure to do this can cause a fate worse than death.)

4. *Leave a physical placeholder in the file cabinet where you removed the file.* (A cardboard strip works well.) This saves you time when refiling the case and it tells someone else the file is out.

5. *Use the copyroom correctly and efficiently.* Select the proper page size and make as few copies as possible; don't forget to refile the original documents with the copies; and don't leave the place a mess.

6. *Don't leave completed files on your desk any longer than necessary.* Refile them as quickly as possible.

7. *Refile the files in their proper places.* New clients, pending settlement cases, pending trial cases, settled cases, and "dead" cases should all go in their respective file drawers.

8. *Protect the files from the usual office hazards.* Keep them away from coffee spills, and prevent accidental loss or damage.

9. *Make sure an assigned person or designated alternate always locks the file cabinets at the end of the work day.*

10. *Aim for a "no lost files" goal for your entire office.*

Even the most organized professionals in the most organized office can slip up. But if you adhere to the rules as closely as possible, you won't spend sleepless hours tossing and turning over the 5,000 possible locations of Mr. Smith's file in your office.

Client Management

The lifeblood of any practicing law office is obviously the clients. Just as no business could function without customers, no law firm could survive without clients. No matter how you want to look at it, clients are customers. More specifically, clients are *your* customers.

Unless complexities of the case or personalities of the clients demand special attention, the attorney or attorneys in your office may speak to clients only a few times over the course of the case. You, on the other hand, may need to speak to the clients constantly, updating them on various matters and advising them of deadlines, appearances, and any progress made in the case. Moreover, since the client's attorney is usually busy with other matters, you may have to take on the role of "point man" for most attorney-client conversations and correspondence.

You've no doubt realized this last part can be very draining, both physically and mentally. Each client expects superior service from your law firm. Each client truly believes his or her case should be the most important one in the office. Furthermore, each client feels that his or her phone calls should be answered promptly by someone who can give a detailed status report or at least some words of comfort about the entire procedure. In short, each client expects to receive special treatment from his or her attorney.

Most new clients will have had few previous encounters with

either attorneys or the legal profession. Short of a traffic accident, a bankruptcy, or a divorce, few people need a lawyer until they *really* need a lawyer. For these inexperienced individuals, even the prospect of visiting a lawyer's office can bring up certain apprehensions. And thanks to Hollywood and television, the image of the typical law office brings to mind visions of stately oak rooms, large intimidating desks, and well-heeled attorneys wearing expensive three-piece suits. Whether or not this is true of your law office, much of the burden of client reassurance may fall on your shoulders. You must be current on the status of the case, be accessible to give information, and even be the hand-holder if necessary.

In his best-selling book *Service America!*, management expert Karl Albrecht tells of a common theme among service workers: "You know," they often say as a group, "this would be a great job if it weren't for all these customers!"

With attorney-client workloads the way they are, it's easy to fall into this same trap. While some paralegals will admit feeling underused if they aren't swamped with work, most express frustration when their workloads get out of control.

Getting control of your workload begins with sorting the priorities. One of the easiest ways to fall behind is to get into a "firefighting" mode, in which you bounce from one crisis to the next trying to deal with minor and major emergencies while the so-called routine cases start to pile up. While some people are proud of their messy desks and their ability to locate a piece of paper instantly even if it's buried under mountains of things, not everyone has a knack for this loose efficiency. In many law firms, senior attorneys will admit that a cluttered, out-of-control desk may mean files that are cluttered and out of control. As the paralegal in charge, *you* are in charge.

Begin at the Beginning

Excellence in client management begins and ends with the file. The files in your office should reflect an overwhelming sense of professionalism, clarity, and above all else, organization. Any qualified member of your office—an attorney, another paralegal, or a secretary—should be able to go to the filing cabinet, find the file he or she needs, and open it with complete confidence that everything will be in its place. The file should be so seamless—with no time gaps or missing forms, memos, letters, etc.—that whoever reviews it will know immediately what will happen next, or better yet, what to do next.

Many successful firms use internal file checklists to keep track of the flow of paper in and out of the file. These lists vary from office to office, but in most firms they relate to the type of case. Tracking needs of cases involving such diverse matters as personal injury, criminal defense, real estate, business contracts, partnerships, or corporations are very different and require different checklists that address those needs.

In paper files, these checklists are attached to the inside left flap and consist of the necessary items to be completed, space for the date the task was completed, and the initials of the completor. As the case nears the settlement or trial stage, an attorney or paralegal can track its progress simply by reviewing the checklist and quickly perusing the file. In a computer file, the checklist comes first, immediately following the caption.

This handy method also prevents embarrassing errors. Since you or the other staffers in your office can't possibly remember the details surrounding every case, the checklist tells you what you've already done. Using a typical personal injury car-accident case, for example, you can review the checklist to track the progress: Our letter to the client's insurance company? Yes, it was sent. Our letter to the defendant's insurance company? Yes, it went out last week. A doctor's lien signed by all parties? Yes. Written estimates and photos of client's damaged car? Yes, attached inside. The defendant's insurance company settlement offer? Received and noted. Tracking sheet of billable hours, i.e., phone time, court time, research time, etc.? Finished and filed. You get the idea.

The checklist prevents you from sending duplicate letters, making unnecessary phone calls, and generally doubling your workload. It also allows you to give accurate briefings to the attorney should he or she need to speak to the client. This can save embarrassment for both of you, as clients will be assured the firm is on top of their cases and they are getting the "white glove/red carpet" treatment they deserve. Other law firms use different-colored files as a way of tracking the progress of each case as the client moves from one legal area to the next. Continuing with the personal injury case, some firms will use red files to indicate a new client (needing to sign representation forms, report requests, medical waivers, etc.); blue files for cases in progress; and green files for settled, "dead," substituted, or otherwise closed cases.

It may sound tedious to change from one file folder color to the next, but in a high-volume law office with several hundred cases, it's an organizational lifesaver. It offers everyone an immediate update for the cases, telling which are new, pending, or complete. It aids your file storage decisions and serves as a constant reminder about the progress of every case in the office.

For more help in organizing the office, the paper flow, and the communication processes, consider this list of allimportant factors— what I call "The Paralegal's Five D Organizing Method."

Ask yourself the following questions every time you encounter a new case, a new problem, new correspondence, puzzling phone calls, or a time management dilemma:

Deadlines—Is the clock ticking?

Ask yourself if any part of the case involves deadlines relating to filing times, court appearances, depositions, hearings, arbitrations, conferences, or settlement offers.

Is this a fast-track case, meaning that any civil or criminal motions have to be filed within a strict court-imposed deadline? Are there any specific deadlines relating to the client? Will he or she be leaving town, going on vacation, moving away completely, etc.?

Ask yourself the same questions about the witnesses and defendants. Is there anything about their movements that may create time conflicts?

How about the attorneys assigned to the case? Do they have conflicting cases or other important court dates? Will they be in town to attend meetings, run depositions, or appear in court?

Finally, consider the many different rules and idiosyncrasies that cover our court system. The rules pertaining to municipal court dates, appearances, and continuances are different from those relating to the superior or appellate courts. The filing deadlines, fees, clerks, and other assorted legal hurdles relating to federal court differ widely from those relating to bankruptcy, probate, or even small claims court.

Keep these variables in mind as you plan the case and as it takes shape. Deadline issues and problems are some of the most serious you will face because lost time invariably means lost money.

Data—Do you need more information?

Can you solve the problem or settle the issue with the information already in front of you? Do you need to do more research in your office or at the law library? Make phone calls? Hire an expert to find the information?

While you're deciding if you need more information, you should ask yourself if you can get that information or start the information-gathering process right now. And if you have the information, can you solve the problem immediately? Time management experts like to espouse the "handle it once" method for solving problems. Can you grasp the problem, discover the solution, and handle it completely, all in the first pass?

If so, do it, because to put it off until later is to add to the original problem. This doesn't mean you should make hasty decisions just to clear your desk but rather that you should try to solve office and case problems as efficiently as possible. We all know people who can take two days to handwrite a half-page memo.

Remember the popular TV show "The Honeymooners"? Jackie Gleason's character would get infuriated as he watched Art Carney's character go through many "warming up" motions just to do some-thing routine, like reading the newspaper. Once you've gathered enough ammunition to solve your problem, don't procrastinate. Fix the problem and move on.

Dollars—Is this a money issue, either for your firm or the client?

Some law offices give their people a spending limit— under $500 means that you can make the decision yourself, and over $500 means that you should seek approval from the powers that be before you act. Whether you have *carte-blanche* or a set dollar limit, you must always consider the financial impact of your decisions upon your firm and your clients.

In many cases, you'll be able to handle routine dollaramount decisions with little or no resistance from your superiors, but in others, it's safer to ask for the go-ahead. This caveat definitely applies to any high money amount that affects the firm's costs system or the client's bottom line, including: retaining potentially high-priced expert witnesses like doctors, investigators, adjusters, and assorted scientific-studies people; scheduling depositions with large numbers of witnesses or defendants; bringing in outside trial attorneys, litigators, or specific legal research subject experts; and spending money to conduct extensive asset searches or to create video evidence, scale models, or aerial photographs.

Any decision involving these kinds of issues should be approved by your boss, the senior staff member, or someone else who can take the responsibility.

Delegate—Can or should you ask someone else to do the work for you?

Start by asking if the problem or task is more suited to someone else in your office. While this may sound like a classic example of buck-passing, it really makes better sense to ask your office-mates to help with projects that may match their level of expertise more than yours.

Needless overwork is the unhappy consequence when a competent individual feels he or she must do every task and couldn't possibly let someone else carry the load. Some people feel irrevocably ruled by the phrase "If you want something done right, do it yourself."

In defending this stance, they may explain that other colleagues have let them down while helping on past projects. While this can affect their feelings, it shouldn't always stand in the way of the delegation process. Noted management and organizational effectiveness experts have always offered the same advice: Find out what the people around you like to do and can do well; then let them do it.

If you work in a large office with other paralegals, you can recognize some work traits almost immediately. Some people like to do legal research, others may enjoy attending depositions, and others may like to handle the peripheral office matters that drive you crazy. Whatever the case, learn to spot colleagues who can take some pressure off you by helping out. No one has asked you to work like a machine. Delegate your chosen projects wisely and let other people help for the common good of the firm.

Decisions—Is this a decision you can make alone?

Most of the important decisions surrounding a case require some thought and some research before you act. Focus on the key issues and ask yourself these questions: How important is the decision? Do I have the authority to make the decision alone? Can I get an answer by talking briefly with the attorney in charge of the case, or do I need to schedule a meeting and give a complete update?

Here are some other factors that may influence the way you make your decisions:

The type of case: Is it a personal injury case? A criminal defense, insurance defense, or worker's compensation case? Does it pertain to real estate, probate, divorce, family law, legal or other professional malpractice, patent law, tax law, wills and trusts law, labor law, environmental law, construction law, finance law, bankruptcy, immigration, corporate and business law, civil litigation, or international law?

Knowing the type of case can point you to the proper attorney, the office expert on the subject, or the firm's research library. If you aren't competent to make the decision, don't.

Client location: Can you contact the client easily? Do you know the client's work schedule, home and work phone numbers, and general availability?

Witness location: Have you identified and located any potential witnesses? Can you contact these people in a short time? Because many civil and criminal cases take literally years to unfold and develop, witnesses can move to other cities and even to other states without your knowledge. Few problems offer more of a legal nightmare than losing witnesses just before important depositions or court appearances. Decide early on if you'll need to keep track of your important witnesses, and if so, establish a procedure and timetable and follow through.

Defendant(s) location: Do you know everything possible about the defendant(s) in the case? Is it a person, a group of people, or an organization? Are there jurisdictional issues within your city or state to consider? Have you started any process service maneuvers? Will you need to serve multiple defendants? If the defendant is a corporation, have you located the agent for service? Have you considered when and how to serve defendant(s)? What is the overall cooperation level of the defendant(s)? Are there any noticeable delaying tactics from the other side that should come to your attorney's attention?

Discovery and evidence availability: Will you need to help prepare for a trial? Are there deadlines, appearances, meetings, and conferences to plan around? What about the existence of any evidence? Will you need to meet with opposing counsel? Conduct private lab tests? Hire professional examiners?

Forms and paperwork: Even the smallest, most matter-of-fact case can generate forests of paper. Do you have "all your ducks in a row" so the attorney can begin to prepare the case for settlement, trial, or final submission of billable hours? Have you reviewed the checklist in the case file for all the appropriate office forms, documentation, correspondence, memos, briefs, court information, depositions, employment records, waivers, medical reports, etc.?

Dollar amounts: Are you aware of the dollar amounts surrounding the case? Are the settlement figures accurate? Can the attorney make informed decisions about the settlement offers, dollar amounts, and related legal fees surrounding the case?

Insurance policy information: Many civil cases revolve around insurance. Who has it? Who doesn't have it? And how much or how little does everyone have? Much of the insurance information–gathering responsibility will fall on your desk. Be sure the client file contains policy numbers, coverages, issue and expiration dates, and dollar limits for everyone involved in the case. Check on the existence of "floaters," homeowner's property coverage, homeowner's personal injury coverage, business liability insurance, errors and omissions insurance, business property insurance, deductibles, and most importantly, issues that relate to quickly repairing the client's personal property damage.

These "Five D's" should help you solve even the most intricate problems. Remember that every case is different; every law firm chooses to do things in its own way; and the people around you are diverse and multifaceted, with their own skills, energies, and talents.

Clients, the attorneys, and the surrounding support staffers all bring their unique perspectives to a problem. As with everything in this book, focus on what applies to you and take what you can from it.

Mentors and Mentoring

As a paralegal professional, your employment entails many diverse duties and responsibilities. Your role largely depends upon the type of law practiced at the office where you work. Small firms may handle any case that comes in the door. Midsize firms may specialize in one kind of law and may in fact be quite well known and successful at it. Larger firms may offer a diverse range of legal services with a bank of specializing attorneys.

Your job duties largely depend on the law firm. Some firms spend a significant amount of time preparing for and completing major trials. Other firms may rarely appear in court, choosing instead to settle nearly every case. And while some firms may handle only business or corporate clients, others may serve clients ranging from megaconglomerates to municipal entities to indigent welfare recipients to undocumented migrant workers.

If your firm is heavily involved in trial work, you'll probably spend most of your time in court, filing writs, briefs, and motions or helping the attorneys prepare for court. In other firms you may be asked to offer administrative support and help run the whole office in a smooth and orderly fashion. You may be asked to offer limited legal assistance to clients in standard divorce cases, bankruptcy, probate, etc.

Some firms hire paralegals strictly to help with legal research. Still others use paralegals mainly in a production role: typing and editing briefs; preparing contracts, wills and trusts; tracking the billable hours for each case; and managing the filing systems.

Whatever your role or duties, the best way to establish yourself as a true paralegal professional is to seek out mentors. The dictionary defines *mentor* as a "wise counselor or loyal advisor." The concept of business mentors has really become popular only in the last ten years. The idea first involved new managers and executives who looked for support, advice, and wisdom from colleagues with more time in the field. Mentor relationships offer younger or less experienced employees a way to learn the system and grow and develop as professionals in a way not unlike the apprentice–journeyman relationship you might find in a construction trade.

In your context, the right mentors can give you careful direction, choice assignments, and even occasional protection during rampages by angry senior partners.

You should look to build two types of mentor relationships, one with an attorney in your firm and (if you work in a firm with a big support staff) one with another paralegal. Each person can help you do your job more effectively by offering advice about the work from his or her own perspective.

The attorney can help you identify the issues to focus on with a particular case, how to solve a complex problem, and most importantly, what the other attorneys need from you for everyone to work more effectively.

Attorney and paralegal mentors can help you understand the corporate culture by offering suggestions concerning office politics, potential "danger zones," and the overall direction of the firm. This information can be priceless for you because the more you know about working effectively with the different personalities in your office, the easier your job will become. Some attorneys want minimum help from you but maximum paperwork in the file. Others may want large amounts of help from you, including research, brief preparation, and trial help. It pays to know how to give the kind of assistance that makes you valuable to individual attorneys and to the firm.

After all, as noted business management expert Harvey Mackay so succinctly points out in his bestselling book *Beware the Naked Man Who Offers You His Shirt*, "If you aren't helping your firm bring in at least as much money as they are paying you, why should they keep you?"

If you work in a large to midsize firm staffed with several paralegals, it helps to choose an appropriate mentor from the group. The best way to begin any mentor relationship is from a position of total honesty. There is nothing wrong or dishonorable about finding an experienced, compatible paralegal colleague and saying, "I like the way you do your work. Can I get some help from you when I have a problem with a case, a client, or someone in the office?"

As with your attorney mentor, your paralegal mentor doesn't have to be your closest friend in the world, your symbolic shoulder to cry on, or the subject of hero worship. You should always maintain a dignified, professional relationship while in the office.

What if you are the senior paralegal in your office? What if everyone comes to you for help and advice? What should this suggest to you? In terms of the paralegal mentor, if you don't have one, be one. Make yourself available to new office staffers, new attorneys, and new paralegals whenever you can. Give advice, give direction, and make yourself completely irreplaceable and invaluable to the firm.

two

INTERVIEWING
TECHNIQUES:
Meeting with
Clients, Witnesses,
and Other Case
Participants

"You never know how much a man can't remember until he is called as a witness."—Laurence Peter

When potential clients first enter the law office where you work, their initial impressions of the firm are influenced by a number of factors, including how they are treated by the front-desk people, how long they wait in the lobby, how they are greeted by the attorney who will handle their case, how politely and skillfully they are interviewed by the attorney, and (if this is part of the package) how well their case is delegated to the paralegal in charge.

What these items have in common relates to a service management concept called the "Moment of Truth" (MOT). By definition, a moment of truth occurs any time a client comes into contact with you or any part of your organization and makes a judgement about the service he or she receives. There are literally thousands of MOTs taking place each time someone does business with a law firm.

With typical service businesses, MOTs are either negative (no towels in the hotel, rude phone clerks, etc.) or positive (a salesperson who calls to tell you about a sale, a free car wash at the car dealership, etc.). You can and should manage these moments to reflect service quality in your office.

Customer satisfaction surveys tell us that if a person receives good service from an organization, he or she will likely tell five to seven people about it. But unfortunately, if a person receives poor service, he or she will likely tell nine to 11 people. Think about your own dealings with service firms like banks, insurance companies, hotels, auto repair shops, etc. If you were served in an efficient, timely, and gracious manner, you enjoyed the encounter and probably would mention it to friends and family. However, if you were mistreated at any of these places, such as by rude frontline employees, long delays, or poor workmanship, you probably would go out of your way to tell friends and family never to do business with that firm.

You work in a service industry, for there is no law firm without clients, and the principles of providing good service are the same as with any typical customer service business. In your own mind (but only in your mind, not in face-to-face contacts), get used to calling clients "customers"; their existence justifies your existence.

The MOT concept is a powerful one. Remember that people have many choices about where to go for legal services. Unless you work for the only attorney in your town, chances are the legal field is crowded with members offering an enormous variety of services for potential clients.

Just as word of mouth is a critical factor with service businesses, i.e., good service begets good word of mouth and bad begets bad, so it goes with law firms.

Marketing studies for attorneys tell us that most people pick an attorney from an ad in the phone book, from a television commercial, or on the recommendations of friends, relatives, or business colleagues. While this may seem a bit haphazard, it should point out that the margin for service errors is slim. If your firm can't or won't offer shining service to its clients, then those clients will go where they can get it.

While you can't control each of the many MOTs that relate to clients, you can monitor the ones that relate specifically to you. In many cases involving such matters as personal injury, worker's compensation, and family law, you'll handle the majority of client conversations that don't come into the scope of the attorney handling the case.

Client Interviews

Let us consider as an example a personal injury or criminal defense case. Many attorneys will handle the initial client interview and then turn the case over to you to begin the standard office procedures that will take it from start to finish. Often if you are to become at all involved, the attorney may call you into the office during this first meeting. While some attorneys will do this for the ceremony of introducing you to the client and the client to a member of the firm's legal staff, others will call you to the meeting so you can become personally familiar with the client and his or her case.

This meeting process can go a long way toward improving your grasp of the specifics of the case and your overall understanding of the many cases that come into the office. If you aren't now a part of the initial or follow-up client interviews and you feel you don't have enough information to process the files effectively, take the initiative to suggest to your attorneys that you attend these meetings.

Using a "Client Profile" sheet, you can fill in all the necessary data—names, addresses, telephone numbers, dates, times, insurance, defendant's name and insurance information, property damage, or arrest date, nature of the arrest, etc.—right on the spot. This can save you time, energy, and wasted phone calls because you can get the data while the client is available with the information you need.

If, on the other hand, you aren't privy to the initial client meetings, you'll obviously need to schedule your own appointment—in person at your office or by telephone—with the client. Because deadlines are nearly always looming no matter what the type of case, make sure you arrange this meeting quickly. Time has a way of spoiling even the best memories. Important documents can get lost, evidence disappears, and the longer you wait, the faster the other side can move ahead.

And bear in mind that in nearly every legal matter there is the other side. Whether it happens to be an insurance company, a State Board, a prosecutor, a business conglomerate, a real estate buyer or seller, or another law firm, this other side is working on many of the same issues as your firm, even if it's in other directions.

Once the client has left the office, it's also a wise idea to stand by and ask for a "marching plan" from the attorney handling the case. This can be as simple as asking if this is a routine case to be handled in a similar fashion as others in the office or if there are extenuating circumstances or special factors relating to time, money, or information you may need to know.

This post-client meeting can serve to pinpoint some of the issues that may become important later. You may need to make a number of immediate and important phone calls to verify information; you may need to do some legal research to see if the firm will want to take the case; or you may want to set any number of other people— legal experts, investigators, data searchers, etc.—in motion to help your position.

If you have been responsible for conducting in-depth interviews with clients, then you probably have developed an information-gathering system that works for you. If so, stick to it and make adjustments in the kinds of questions and in the way you gather the information as necessary. If you don't have much experience in client, witness, or defendant interviewing techniques, then review the following section with your own caseload in mind. Some of the questions of course won't apply exactly to the cases in your office, and some won't relate to the type of law practiced by your attorneys. Still, you'll notice from the flow of the questions how it is possible to gather most of the information you'll need in just a short period of time.

What follows is a primer on interviewing techniques. As always, take what works for you and create your own standard client or witness questionnaires to match your needs. Even if you ask the same questions time after time and even if you feel you know them by heart, consider devising some type of standard questionnaire to help you remember to ask everything the first time. If you don't already use a written list, simply create one to fit the type of case you're handling.

Interviewing a client is usually a smooth process. In most cases, clients are receptive to your questions because they usually recognize the importance of cooperation for the success of the case. However, keep in mind that even though most clients want to help you, they may feel uncomfortable about being in an attorney's office.

People usually deal with attorneys only when something is wrong or up in the air—an injury, a lawsuit, a bankruptcy, a divorce, a criminal charge, probate, a lease deal, etc. They may feel particularly intimidated when they first arrive at an attorney's office, especially if it's filled with expensive art, furniture, or law books, like law offices they've seen in the movies or on TV.

Remember to make the client feel welcome and comfortable. Going to an attorney is a matter of choice. If it's not you, it could be someone else. Always remember that clients are really customers and deserve special treatment.

Once the client is with you, be aware of typical conversation barriers, like a large desk, that can inhibit the flow of communication. Sit face to face if you can, without a big desk in front of you. If both of you sit across a small table, you can still take notes, but it doesn't feel so daunting.

Sample Client Interview Questions

Using a common personal injury car-accident client as an example, consider the following list of questions for your next client interview:

1. What was the date and time of the accident?

2. Where did the accident happen? Freeway? Surface streets?

3. In what direction was the client going?

4. In what direction was the other driver going?

5. Was weather or darkness a factor in the accident?

6. Is there a police report?

7. If so, by what agency? Local police? Sheriff? State Highway Patrol?

8. If not, why not?

9. What did the officer say to the client?

10. What did the officer say to the other driver?

11. How many cars were involved in the accident?

12. How many people were involved in the accident?

13. Any pedestrians? Small children? Motorcycle or bike riders?

14. What kind of car was the client driving?

15. Who owns the car?

16. Who insures the car? (Company, policy number, agent, etc.)

17. How did the accident happen? Rear-end? Broadsided on the driver or passenger side? Head-on collision? Side-swipe?

18. How much damage was done to the car?

19. Does the client have a damage estimate yet?

20. Has the client notified his or her insurance company? The Department of Motor Vehicles?

21. What kind of car was the defendant driving?

22. Who owns the defendant's car?

23. Who insures the defendant's car? (Company, policy number, agent, etc.)

24. How much damage was done to the defendant's car?

25. Did the defendant make any statements or admit fault?

26. Were there any witnesses?

27. Does the client have any witness names and telephone numbers?

28. Does the client have any photos of the accident scene or either vehicle?

29. Can the client make a brief diagram of the scene?

30. How was the client injured in the accident?

31. Did the client seek treatment after the accident?

32. Does the client have medical payment coverage?

33. Does the client have a family doctor?

34. Has the client lost time from work because of the accident?

35. Has the client been in any other accidents?

While this isn't the most complete questionnaire on the subject, it does cover most of the critical information you'll need to begin working on the case.

You'll notice that some of the questions lead into others and others get answered during the discussions. If you find this list helpful and aren't already using a preprinted version of it, consider creating a similar questionnaire to handle the personal injury auto-accident cases that come to your office.

You can modify this questionnaire to cover most slip-and-fall accidents, worker's compensation accidents, or other injury- or insurance-related incidents.

Continuing with our client interview questions, let's assume now that the client you need to interview was arrested on a criminal charge. Here are some questions you may want to ask:

1. What was the date and time of arrest?

2. What are the charges?

3. Which law enforcement agency made the arrest? Local police? Sheriff? State Highway Patrol?

4. Does the client have a copy of the police report yet?

5. What chemical tests (if any) did the client submit to? Breath? Blood? Urine?

6. What are the results of those tests?

7. Did the police impound any evidence, like the client's car?

8. Was the client injured in the arrest process?

9. If so, was the client treated at a local hospital?

10. Was the client booked into jail or released with a citation?

11. If so, when is the court date?

12. Did the client make bail?

13. Were any of the client's friends at the scene?

14. Are there any independent witnesses to the crime or arrest?

15. What were the circumstances of the arrest?

16. What probable cause did the officer(s) use, i.e., the reason for the original stop and contact?

17. Was the client arraigned?

18. If so, under what charges?

19. Does the client have a prior criminal history?

20. Is the client on parole or probation?

The questions should give you a good place to start during the criminal defense client interview process. Other questions will surely come to mind as you talk to the client.

After taking careful notes of the client's answers and remarks, you should thank him or her for coming in and promise to get in touch again very soon. You can imagine how apprehensive a client can feel after a car accident, an arrest, or a worker's compensation accident, or with a large business, real estate, or family law matter on the line.

After some time in your profession, one case begins to look like any other. While it may feel like that to you and to the other attorneys and paralegals in the office, the case is unique and is definitely of significance to the client. His or her physical or mental health, freedom, business future, or family life may be riding on the outcome of the case.

Keep the importance of each case in the back of your mind at all times. What seems routine and standard to you can be mind-boggling and frightening to the client. Most people unfamiliar with our legal system can find the process of working with a lawyer to be highly intimidating.

Most people come to a law office in a high degree of emotion. They may be suffering from the ill effects of a highly stressful family problem, personal injury, business catastrophe, recent death of a loved one, immigration problem, or criminal matter. Try to provide some small amount of comfort, at least by offering your sympathy when it seems necessary, and the promise of support from you and your firm.

This is not to say you should live and die with every case, pouring your emotions into every "shaggy-dog" story that comes into the office, but rather, that you keep a balanced perspective concerning the importance of the case to all the participants—clients, defendants, witnesses, etc.

Some people merely want to hear you say, "Our firm understands your case very well. We've handled a number of similar cases and we've had good results. Your attorney has a strong background in these types of cases and will know what to do for you."

A few statements of encouragement from you (along with the attorney) can go a long way toward improving the client's peace of mind. This can create good feelings all around, meaning better communication between the client and the firm, an easier path to settling the case, and with luck, a helpful referral to other potential clients in the future.

After your first interview meeting with the client, try to schedule a short meeting with the attorney handling the case. This is a good time to bring up any questions or concerns you might have, and it offers an opportunity to ask for some directions. The attorney may want you to tackle certain problems surrounding the case, make special phone calls, start researching critical issues, or just handle the case in a manner similar to the way you handled others in the past.

These initial attorney-paralegal meetings can last from one minute to one hour, depending on the complexity of the case and other time pressures. Make sure you feel comfortable with your role in the case before you leave.

Back at your desk, you should already be planning your next moves: start a new client file, organize your notes from the client interview, make a list of the phone calls you'll need to make, draft various letters, make calendar notations, etc.

Before you plunge ahead on any case handed to you, stop and get a feel for it. If it's a new case, review your notes and organize a plan of attack. If it's an ongoing case, read the file, read the reports and other significant documentation, and review the memos, briefs, and correspondence before you do anything else. Look things over carefully to avoid future embarrassments, mistakes, or repetitions.

Interviewing Basics

Some law firms ask their paralegals to initiate and conduct all witness interviews for accident, criminal, and similar cases. In these instances, you'll want to follow some careful guidelines to avoid any problems later (when they're usually too large to fix). Using paralegals saves money, and many firms like to give their staffs the chance to track the case from start to finish.

Other firms rely on outside or in-house investigators to handle witness statements. You must defer to the wishes of your firm. Good investigators can quickly take a number of witness statements and give you the information within days instead of weeks. You'll get a good idea of how to utilize this valuable resource in Chapter 4.

If you're called on to do any witness interviews, you should start by taking a close look at the way you listen to people. While this may sound like teaching the choir to sing, interviewing is a high-skill activity.

For the majority of us, the opposite of talking is not listening, but waiting to talk again. Learn to listen "actively" by paraphrasing what the other person has said and filling in what you don't know, e.g., "Mr. Jones, if I heard you correctly, what you said was . . . ."

Active Listening

1. Be open and receptive with your body language.

2. Hear all of what the other person says before you respond.

3. Don't interrupt or finish sentences for the other person.

4. Interpret the other person's message by listening for feelings as well as facts.

5. Act on what he or she has said.

Before you even start any client or witness interview session, develop your paraphrasing skills.

Paraphrasing, according to "Verbal Judo" seminar leader George Thompson, "is a necessary backup system to communication. It means putting the other person's 'meaning' into your 'words' and then giving it back to him."

This technique of replaying what the other person has said and putting it into your own words can pay powerful dividends during any interview. It will help you build immediate rapport with the person.

Paraphrasing allows you to get the information right the first time. The other person can correct you if you've made an error, and the paraphrased statement makes him or her feel better because it mirrors what he or she originally said to you.

"It also," says Thompson, "makes the other person a better listener to you. No one will listen harder than to his or her own point of view."

Paraphrasing also has a tendency to create an aura of empathy with your client's case because the person will believe you are really trying to understand what happened.

Witness Interviews

Interviewing witnesses requires the same amount of careful preparation as interviewing clients, if not more so. Make a list of your questions before you begin, focusing on the ones that pertain to the actions of your client and the nature of the case. Try to establish exactly where the witness was and what, if anything, he or she saw your client actually do.

Read over your initial interview with the client to see if there are any discrepancies. In some cases, you'll need to ask the witness to clarify important details the client forgot to tell you. Also review any additional outside information, like police accident or arrest reports, before you begin. Look at photos, diagrams, maps, etc., to get a feel for the case. A small amount of preparation in the beginning will save time and effort for both you and the witness and will help you get an accurate and complete statement of who did what to whom and why.

The key to any successful witness interview lies in your ability to help the witness paint his or her own word picture of the event in question. Simple "yes" and "no" questions followed by "yes" and "no" answers won't help you very much. Strive to get the most accurate portrayal of the actions and activities that took place.

How much witnesses will tell you depends upon a number of key factors that are usually out of your control, including their eyesight levels; how near or far away they were at the time of the incident; their relationship (if any) with the client or the defendant in the case; their perception of the entire incident as a whole (unconcerned, worried about the client, worried about the defendant); hostility toward anyone involved; and last, but most important, their willingness to get involved in the case.

Some people are naturally gregarious and want to help you in any way they can. Others are more reticent and will only help if gently prodded. Other witnesses can be highly uncooperative and even downright hostile if they do not want to get involved in the matter. But of all the factors that relate to whether or not a witness is helpful to your case, the only one you can control with any certainty is the witness's positive feelings toward *you* as a person.

It only makes sense: people will usually go out of their way to help people they like, and conversely, will not do anything to help people they don't.

Case in point: If you're trying to interview a person who witnessed a car accident involving your client and another driver, you can inadvertently alienate him or her with your first (and probably only) phone call.

Before you pick up the telephone to contact a witness, think for a moment about how many other inquiries he or she has probably received prior to your call. Most insurance companies encourage their adjusters to get witness statements immediately. They do this first because fresh information is best and because they want to beat the other side—attorneys, investigators, or paralegals working for the other driver—to the punch.

Fortunately for you, most insurance adjusters are so swamped with cases that they don't always have the time (or energy) to get to your witness. Still, in many cases, by the time the client comes to your law firm and meets with an attorney, several days or even weeks might have passed. Most people are hesitant to go to a personal injury lawyer unless their injuries are severe or a friend or family member encourages them to do so.

If any serious length of time has passed, you can almost bet your witness has been inundated with phone calls by the other driver's insurance company, the other driver's attorney (if one exists), and even the police, if the case is significant enough. And keep in mind that most of these calls have probably interrupted his or her work day or home life. For most people, getting a phone call from an attorney's paralegal, an insurance investigator, or a private investigator during their work day or the dinner hour ranks right up there with calls from people who sell aluminum siding, penny stocks, or tap water purifying systems.

Unfortunately, many people often end up wishing they had not gotten involved in the incident in the first place, and they vow to "see nothing" and offer no help should they ever witness another incident. Telling the same story over and over to six or seven people doesn't make for a fun evening. Keep this in mind if you're asked to interview any witnesses for a case—personal injury, worker's compensation, crime, etc. Concentrate on following two key rules: Get to them first, and be as polite as humanly possible at all times.

In a busy law office, the telephone can be your best information-gathering tool. With some well-placed phone calls, you can take statements, verify information, and generally handle large portions of an entire case without leaving the comfort of your office. Since few witnesses would actually think about journeying to an attorney's office just to give information on behalf of a total stranger, it makes sense to get this information by phone. It keeps scheduling problems to a minimum and offers an efficient communication method for both the interviewer and the witness.

By reaching any potential witnesses before the other side, you reap the obvious advantages of hearing the story first while it's fresh and before any antagonism sets in because the witness has been plagued with so many calls.

The politeness factor is a given. Even the most hardboiled, cranky, and tired-of-telling-it witness will respond if you are polite and professional on the phone. Above all else, be liberal in your use of the phrase "thank you again for helping us get to the bottom of this case." People want to know they're making a contribution and it feeds their egos to think that without them you would be stuck for answers. So make them think their help is invaluable; in many cases it is.

The Important Witness

Review the following car accident personal injury episode and notice the important part played by the witness:

About 9:00 one night, Party Three (P-3) is stopped at the limit line of a traffic signal, waiting for her light to turn green. Party Two

(P-2) is directly behind her, about one-half car length away. Party One (P-1) is in the lane behind P-2 and not paying much attention to his driving or his rate of speed. He looks up to see P-2's rear bumper a few yards away. He slams on the brakes, skids for a short distance and smacks into the back of P-2's car. P-2 slides forward and crashes into the rear of P-3's bumper.

Each driver gets out to look at the damage, and everyone agrees to pull into a nearby gas station lot to wait for the police. A station employee saw the entire accident from where he stood and agrees to give a witness statement. The police arrive on the scene and, after verifying that no one is injured, begin to interview the participants. This is where the fun starts.

The next morning Party Three wakes up and notices her neck is stiff and sore. Her left shoulder is tender to the touch and she has a slight headache. She has trouble putting her clothes on because of this stiffness. She goes out to her driveway and looks at the back of her car. She sees a good-sized dent in her rear bumper, along with some chrome damage and paint transfer. She goes back into her house and makes two calls: one to her insurance company and one to her attorney.

Party Two wakes up with the same pains in his neck and head. He sees similar damage to his front and rear bumpers, and he makes similar phone calls to his insurance company and attorney.

Party One feels fine except for the hood-bending damage to his car. He makes one phone call: to his insurance company to tell it about his misfortune. However, in this scenario, Party One is already in the high-risk insurance group. He's had several tickets and a few accidents, and his insurance rates are in the upper stratosphere. The version he tells his insurance company differs just a bit from the truth.

In his account of the crash, the SECOND car at the light hit the car ahead of him FIRST; then he came along and just happened to hit the back of the second car. So instead of being on the hook for two smashed cars, he's only admitting to rear-ending the middle one, after it had already hit the car in front.

Parties Two and Three tell their attorneys and insurance companies exactly how the accident happened. P-2 felt two impacts: one for the initial crash and the second after he hit the car ahead of him. P-3 felt one impact when P-2 hit her from behind. But she HEARD the first crash and braced for the impact that followed.

Each attorney and each insurance company requests a copy of the police Traffic Collision report. Once they review it, they discover Mr. Witness working at the gas station near the scene. Immediately, attorneys' paralegals, accident investigators, and insurance adjusters spring into action. Mr. Witness, and his version of the crash, clearly become the key to the whole case.

Everyone tracks Mr. Witness to his work and home and interrupts his work and TV time with requests for his version of the facts. He tells the same story all four times. The adjusters, investigators, paralegals, and attorneys then get in line and hammer heavy financial blows down upon devious P-1 and his insurance company.

Therein lies the moral to this tale: A good witness can save a potentially bad case.

What would have been the result of this case had the parties not interviewed the witness? One participant would have surely started a huge shouting match with another. Accusations would have flown from party to party with each insurance company and attorney siding with its client.

Phone Interviews

Good telephone etiquette can make the difference between getting some information from a cooperative, helpful witness and getting no information from an uncooperative, even hostile witness. Try to schedule your calls to the workplace early in the day before witnesses become immersed in their work, immediately after lunch before they begin working again, and between 5:00 and 6:00 p.m. before they sit down to dinner at home. Check that the time is convenient for the witness. If not, make an appointment for a telephone conversation later that same day.

Use the beginning of the phone call to explain politely who you are, where you work, and what information you seek from the witness. Reiterate how important the statement is to you and be sure to be effusive in your thanks. Make witnesses feel useful and helpful by using your active listening skills to the fullest (i.e., wait for them to finish, don't interrupt, make them feel you understand what they said by paraphrasing and repeating it, etc.).

Once the pre-interview conversation is over, make sure you immediately clarify where the witness was standing when the accident happened and more importantly, whether he or she actually saw the accident or merely heard it. This is a critical distinction because only "eyewitnesses" hold up in court or deposition, not "earwitnesses."

Here, you'll need to decide how you will document the witness statement. There are a few choices, ranging from the inexpensive and error-prone to the expensive and time-consuming.

The worst way to take a witness statement over the phone (or if by some chance you can encourage the witness to visit your office) is by hand, scribbling down your questions and his or her answers on a legal pad as you go. It's cheap, but it's usually chock-full of omissions, errors, and misstatements.

The only exception to this rule comes into play if you can take excellent, reliable, error-free shorthand. Some paralegals are highly skilled at this nearly lost art and can take down an entire witness statement verbatim. If you aren't that skilled, don't try it. There are few worse feelings in the world than having a witness statement disallowed as evidence in a deposition, hearing, or other court proceeding because it's completely inaccurate.

If you plan to take shorthand notes as you talk, make sure you take the time to get direct quotes from the witness, especially since you'll want the witness to sign a copy of his or her transcribed statement later on.

One key point about taking witness statements in person, either at your office or at an outside location with the witness: make sure you indicate in your notes that at the time of the interview, the witness "spoke good English, understood my questions, and appeared lucid and sober."

This statement will protect you later should the other side seek to discredit the witness for some reason. This frequently comes into play when the witness is not a native English speaker and the other side wants to show that he or she did not understand the questions being asked.

In the majority of cases, you'll probably take witnesses' statements over the phone. The best way to take a phone statement (or even an in-person statement) is to use a tape recorder. In these days of the always-changing, newfangled electronic gadget, it is possible to use a high-quality speaker phone coupled with a microcassette recorder to capture an entire statement with relative ease. Transcribing the statements later using a dictation machine can shave many hours off an otherwise dreary task.

Remember that a transcription does not include every cough, "huh," or "you know." A transcribed statement should look and sound like a normal conversation with all of the extraneous background noises and remarks taken out.

If you plan to use a cassette recorder to tape witness statements directly from the telephone, make sure you carefully follow a few important rules:

- Use only the best telephones and recorders your firm can afford. A good speaker phone helps you understand the witness and vice versa. Many of the inferior ones sound as though you're both talking from inside a cave. Choose a high-quality recorder specifically made for dictation. Clear tapes help the person transcribing the tapes (or you) understand the entire conversation on both sides. Remember to speak slowly and clearly into the tape.

- Ask the witness before you start taping if it's acceptable to tape the conversation. If he or she says "yes," tell the witness you're going to put on the speaker phone and ask again for permission to record.

- Using the speaker phone, start your recorder and document the date and time, e.g., "This is Paralegal Jones on February 22, 1992, approximately 5:00 p.m. I'm speaking with Mr. John Smith. Can you hear me okay, Mr. Smith?" Wait for Mr. Smith's affirmative reply before you proceed.

- Ask the witness, "Is it okay with you if I tape-record our conversation?" and then wait for his or her affirmative reply.

- Begin the interview by reviewing the facts surrounding the case. "As I understand it, Mr. Smith, you witnessed an accident on January 25th, 1992, involving a blue Ford truck and a white Chevy Nova, at the intersection of Grape and Maple Streets, at around 3:00 p.m. in the afternoon. Is that correct?"

- Wait for the witness to answer, in case he or she makes any corrections in your information. Not surprisingly, witnesses often know more about the incident than the client because they weren't caught up in the moment or overcome by stress, injury, or other debilitating factors.

- Let the interview go along relatively uninterrupted. In most instances, once the witness gets rolling, your part of the conversation will consist of brief questions that verify specific points and help the witness stay on track about the case.

- Stay in control of the interview. Don't let the witness go off on a tangent, talking about issues that don't relate to the case.

Continuing with the personal injury car-accident example, let's create a line of questioning for you to follow should you need to interview a witness to your client's case.

At the start of this chapter, I gave you some specific questions to ask your client in terms of his or her involvement in a personal injury case. Client statements tend to be quite similar, so you can follow this client question format without much revision. Witness statements, on the other hand, tend to be unique. You have to formulate the questions as they arise and let the story flow. Make sure you do the following:

- Ask the witness to be as specific as possible about the time of the accident. Some crashes occur right at daybreak or dusk, and the use or non-use of headlights may be a notable visibility factor for each party.

- Get all available personal information from each witness, including home and business addresses, home and business phone numbers, date of birth, driver's license number, Social Security number, etc. You or an investigator hired by your firm may need to find these witnesses a number of years after the original crash.

- Ask what happened to each car after the crash. Whose car was towed and why?

- Ask if the witness knows the actual posted speed limit for the street in question. Insurance people and opposing attorneys can have a field day arguing over speed limits. Can the witness pinpoint the location of the controlling speed limit sign?

- Ask the witness about the location and extent of damage (none, minor, major, totaled) to each car. Could there have been old damage someone might try to pawn off as fresh? Does the damage done to each car seem to match what happened in the accident?

- Ask the witness to describe the surrounding area, including the position of the traffic signals, the size and shape of the lanes, the width of the intersections—especially if they're offset—and the type of lane dividers (dots, painted lines, concrete barriers, etc.). Ask if either driver crossed a simulated island before the crash, drove in the bike lane or across construction barricades, etc.

- Ask the witness if he or she remembers the position and use of safety belts or helmets for all passengers and injured parties. Some people can recall who was wearing a seat belt and who was not and will tell you if you ask. Pinpoint who was sitting in which seat in all vehicles involved. This will prevent a nasty version of "musical chairs" later in court, where one person says HE was in the front seat and another person swears HE was, with no one to corroborate either side.

- Does the witness remember noticing (before the crash) any vehicle defects that may have influenced the crash, e.g., no front headlights, wipers, turn signals, or a badly cracked windshield, that may have had an impact on the cause of the accident?

• Ask about the weather, road conditions, and lighting at the time of the crash. Have the witness describe how heavy the fog was or how hard it was raining. Ask if there were any obstructions in the road. This information can go a long way towards affixing the final blame for the accident later on.

• Ask if the witness recalls if all the traffic signals were working at the time of the crash. Sometimes out of the blue, the witness will say, "Oh, no. That signal breaks down all the time. City maintenance crews were working on it a week before the accident." This line of questioning may help to establish the credibility of your witness. The city should have maintenance records for the area and you might want to subpoena this information for a deposition or trial.

• See if the witness remembers anything about the sobriety of each driver or injured passengers or pedestrians. This can help (or hurt) your case, especially if the other driver was arrested for driving under the influence.

• Ask the witness if he or she remembers any injuries or complaints of pain from all parties. Specify who complained of stiff necks, shoulders, and backs, or had bruising injuries, and which car they were in. This verification may prevent "phantom" injuries from appearing months after the accident.

Finally, ask the witness to review the actions and reactions of all witnesses, and the actions and reactions of any other participants in the case, like the police or the defendant. Many times witnesses hear one driver or the other, or the police, make statements that can help or hurt the client's case. Better to hear these sooner rather than later in court.

When you finish the tape-recorded interview, tell the witness, "Okay, Mr. Smith, I'm going to stop the tape now. Are there any subjects I missed or is there anything else you want to add before I stop the tape?"

If the witness wants to add more, continue the interview and repeat the closing statement again. If not, end the interview by inserting the perjury statement: "Do you declare under penalty of perjury and under the laws of (*your state*) that the statement you just gave me is true and correct to the best of your knowledge?"

Once the witness answers positively, end the interview by saying, "It's now approximately X o'clock. I'm going to stop the tape."

Always thank your witnesses again for their participation and add that you'll be sending a typed copy of the conversation to review, sign, and return to you. After you've transcribed the conversation, mail the witness his or her statement to sign and include a self-addressed stamped envelope for his or her convenience.

Defendant Conversations

What about trying to talk with the defendant in the case? Frankly, your chances of talking with the defendant in a civil or criminal case are quite slim. Most people follow the instructions of their insurance company or attorney, who tells them, "DON'T talk to anyone but me about the case."

However, the old saying "It never hurts to ask" may apply in some unique cases. I've talked to the defendant in several important cases and learned information that saved my attorney considerable time, expense, and effort. Who knows what will happen? You may find out that your client is not being truthful; this is definitely information you'll want to pass on to your attorney.

If you do decide to talk with the defendant in a case, DO NOT use false pretenses to worm your way into a conversation. Besides being unethical, in most states it's illegal as well. Never say you're anyone other then yourself. You could find yourself in an embarrassing situation if your attempt at skullduggery gets discovered. The potential looms for a large malpractice suit against your firm (naming you as the defendant), fines, a possible jail sentence, and most assuredly, termination from your job.

If you decide you want to contact defendants in a case, follow the same rules as with other case participants and witnesses: Get to them first and be polite. They may want to tell you their side of the story even when they know you work for the other side. Offer them the chance to "set the record straight" and respectfully ask for their permission to tape-record the conversation.

Interviewing defendants can be hazardous. Once they realize what they have said and to whom, most defendants will swear you tricked them and say they didn't know who they were talking to or why. They will swear their statement is inaccurate, misquoted, or worse, completely fabricated by you. Tread lightly in this area. If you don't feel comfortable contacting the defendant in a case, don't do it. If you can reach a defendant before he or she has been advised to be quiet, you may get some valuable information. If not, don't press the issue; concentrate on helping your case with good client and witness interviews.

Signed Statements

The old saying about something "not being worth the paper it's printed on" certainly holds true for witness (and defendant) statements. An unsigned statement probably won't hold up in any court-related hearing. Without a signature at the bottom, with acknowledgment that the statement was made under penalty of perjury, a statement takes on a contrived, even duplicitous look. Strive to get all of your statements signed by every person you interview.

Once you've transcribed your statements, repeat the "penalty of perjury" paragraph at the end and leave room for the signature and date. Always provide a self-addressed, stamped envelope when you mail a statement to someone. Make it easy for respondents to cooperate with you. Would you be in a hurry to send something back to a law office if you had to hunt for an envelope, the address, and a stamp? Probably not. Offer maximum courtesy to others, and you'll almost always get your statements back signed and on time.

On those rare occasions in which you've taken a statement and not received the signed reply, wait at least seven days before calling the person again. Identify yourself first and ask politely if he or she received the statement you sent. In some cases, the person has misplaced the form, and you must send a duplicate. In other cases, the individual has neglected to mail it, and needs a little prodding to review it and send it back.

Sometimes, however, a person will have second thoughts after reviewing the statement and not want to return it. This reluctance may stem from a sense of uneasiness about having gotten involved in the case in the first place or from a mistaken fear about being dragged into court over the matter. He or she may also have received "helpful" but wrong advice from friends or colleagues about signing anything that looks legal.

If you have witnesses who balk about signing their statements, explain to them that in many cases, a signed statement takes the place of the witness in a court hearing. By signing the statements, they may be able to avoid any other participation in the case. Suggest that if they don't want to sign their statements, they may then have to appear at a hearing to verify what they said on tape.

In those rare instances where a witness persistently refuses to sign, you can't do much except save the tape as evidence of the conversation and proceed with the case. You may be able to subpoena the witness later and use the taped statement as a refresher for him or her.

Some people will flatly tell you they do not want to give a taped statement about the incident. If you feel you have some rapport with them, you might try suggesting an alternative to the taped statement: the question and answer sheet. Tell the witness you'll send a prepared questionnaire form, and all he or she will need to is write down the answers, sign the bottom and mail it back to you. If the witness agrees to this format you can use the questionnaire as your ace in the hole. Why? Because you can create the questionnaire to fit the client's case.

Instead of using a "one size fits all" questionnaire, write yours to match the type of case. For a car-accident case, you might want to use the opening paragraph to give the facts, i.e., date, time, location, drivers' names, and types of cars. By labeling each participant with his or her vehicle, you can create a questionnaire based on the movements of the cars. "Which direction was the blue Ford going?," "Which direction was the white Chevy going?," "Where did the blue Ford hit the white Chevy?" etc.

If your firm specializes in personal injury car-accident cases, you can create a "boilerplate" questionnaire by using your computer's word processor, changing the streets, times, and cars as necessary. Some people feel more comfortable with pre-printed forms on which they can write their own responses, draw diagrams if necessary, and generally choose their words and thoughts more carefully. Remember to include a self-addressed, stamped envelope to speed the reply back to you.

Since any taped statements you take have evidentiary value, you'll need to establish a storage system to protect the actual tapes. Since the signed statement will usually go straight into the client's file, you can place the cassette tape (one statement per tape) in a sealed envelope, mark it with the date, time, client's name, and witness name, and attach it securely to the file. Or you can set aside one lockable file cabinet drawer as an evidence bin, filing the sealed tape envelopes by the client's name. The choice depends upon the size of the office and the number of tapes you plan to collect.

No matter whom you interview—clients, witnesses, defendants, other case participants—be professional in all you do. A confident, mature attitude and the desire to build rapport and actively listen to the other person can go a long way towards learning the truth.

three

"The Lord Chief Justice of England recently said that the greater part of his judicial time was spent investigating collisions between vehicles, each on its own side of the road, each sounding its horn, and each not moving."—Philip Guedalla

*C*ontrary to what you see on television or at the movies, police officers don't spend all their time fighting crime. In fact, they actually spend very little of their time in a crime-fighting mode. It's not for lack of trying, it's just that their workload is too heavy, and their time is taken up by a number of less exciting but equally necessary tasks.

Hollywood likes to show us perfect TV cops who spend every waking hour chasing bad guys, making dozens of felony arrests, and solving major crime cases singlehandedly.

Unfortunately, this is not really how the job goes. Studies of law enforcement tell us the average patrol officer probably spends only 20 percent of his or her patrol day actually in an enforcement position. The rest of the time police officers answer citizen complaints, questions, and requests; write reports; participate in administrative or training tasks; or just drive around their beats waiting for the radio to give them an assignment.

The 20-percent figure that relates to law enforcement—issuing citations, making arrests, and protecting life and property—is certainly an important part of their job as police officers, but it's really only one of their functions.

Many metropolitan cities have created police "ride-along" programs. In these, ordinary citizens can spend a patrol shift with a police officer. This experience can be quite an eye-opener, especially for people who have no prior knowledge of what police officers actually do. Between the crackling sounds of the never-quiet radio to the adrenaline rush of driving fast to one "hot" call after the other, it seems as if you never have a chance to catch your breath.

This ride-along program has gone a long way to help educate the public about what police officers do and why they do it. When interviewed afterward, even the most jaded citizens will admit a newfound, if grudging, respect for the police force.

What many people discover—and what most officers will admit—is that the police spend a good deal of their time writing. For an outdoor job that requires upper-body strength, stamina, and a certain sense of fearlessness, police officers use ballpoint pens far more than guns. While this may sound like a sweeping generalization, it rings true. Few professions require their members to spend so much time documenting their activities on paper.

Police officers must account for nearly every minute of their shift on a daily journal form. This journal tells supervisors when their officers left the station, where they went, what they did in terms of police enforcement activity, when they returned to the station, and even when and where they took a meal break. Nearly every time a police officer climbs out of a patrol car to do anything, some form of activity will appear in the officer's daily journal.

Why such careful scrutiny? Because the police profession is one of the most independent and powerful jobs there is. In a nutshell, a city or county municipality gives each officer it hires a badge, a gun, and a patrol car, and says, "Go out alone and protect us."

Police officers have very little actual supervision over what they do. No one tells them whom to stop or where to go, except during those occasions when the radio dispatcher gives them a call. In between calls, officers can enforce the law as strictly or as leniently as they feel like. It's one of the few professions that demands error-free work all the time—because the decisions officers make can relate to life and death issues, legal matters, or personal freedoms—and yet offers such unsupervised autonomy.

But while police officers are given nearly free rein to do their jobs as they think best, they are also expected to document their activities and their responses to public service calls on a continuous basis. Most officers who retire medically do so because of ailments related to their hearts, backs, and knees. But if you were to take an unofficial poll of working patrol officers, I'm sure the most common affliction among them would be writer's cramp! Even the simplest "routine" report may take one hour or more to complete.

Some officers may write one or two reports a week and others may have to complete three or four lengthy ones per shift. The number and type of reports usually relate to the area of town where the officer works (high-crime or not), the size of the city or county, and the value the officer's supervisors and commanders place upon paperwork. Some police departments require their officers to write volumes of reports, covering even minor incidents like a stolen bicycle or a lost dog. Other departments are not so particular, and their apparent nonchalance about report-taking may have more to do with antiquated record-keeping systems than with lazy police administrators. From your standpoint as a paralegal, the more complete the records and the more up-to-date, efficient systems the better.

If you're curious, here's a short list of the variety of police reports an officer might need to take:

Arrest reports
Crime case reports
Traffic collision reports
Hit-and-run reports
Driving Under the Influence reports
Under the Influence of Controlled Substance reports
Runaway juvenile reports
Found property reports
Stolen vehicle reports
Recovered stolen vehicle reports
Impounded vehicle reports
Death case reports

Attempted suicide reports
Officer-involved traffic collision reports
City-equipment–involved traffic collision reports
Damaged city equipment reports
Injured or dead animal reports

Police Report Quality

Like people in other professions, police officers are human beings with personal likes and dislikes about their jobs. Police report writing offers no exception. Some officers enjoy writing reports, carefully documenting their activities, painting "word pictures" of the events, and adding their own distinctive style and trademark to their efforts. Officers of this type can quickly establish a good reputation among the people who read police reports all day—police supervisors, city and district attorneys, judges, defense attorneys, etc.

Other officers, however, don't particularly enjoy writing reports, and their distaste for this work is evident on the pages they complete. Poor reports—with missing or incomplete information, poor interviewing or investigation procedures, and a sense of shoddy "word-smithing"—will haunt officers just as good reports will help their writers.

Just as good report writers develop a reputation among their colleagues, so do bad report writers. In some cases, prosecuting attorneys will even fail to "issue" or bring the case to court (even if they can win it) because of inferior reports. Officers who turn in poor-quality reports do more harm to their careers than they realize.

What many officers fail to recognize is that a police report, no matter how mundane it seems, serves as a public record. Because the wheels of our criminal justice system turn so slowly, some criminal and civil cases involving the police can go on for years and years, bouncing from one appeals court to the other. The report that documents these cases must be good enough to stand the test of time.

One single arrest report can go from the city prosecutor's office all the way to the United States Supreme Court. That report will carry that officer's name on it wherever it goes. Hundreds of people may read it and make pointed comments about its accuracy, content, style, and overall appearance. That's why police officer recruits are taught from their first day in the academy: "Write each and every report as if your career depended upon it; it just might."

Types of Police Reports

Every police officer in the country will readily admit that given a choice, he or she would rather write an arrest report than any other type. Most officers like these because the end product of an arrest report could mean that someone who belongs there goes to jail. One main complaint about police work as a profession is that there is very little "closure." This means that officers rarely get to see the fruits of their labors come full circle. Once they have written a burglary report or most other types of crime reports, they are out of the picture. They never find out what happened. Did the detectives solve the case? Was a suspect later arrested, tried, and convicted? These are questions that rarely get answered satisfactorily. A morale-building aspect of writing arrest reports is the intense feeling of job satisfaction; someone who did something wrong gets his or her freedom taken away, at least temporarily.

On the other hand, burglary reports, traffic collision reports, non-injury hit-and-runs, and petty crime cases involving juveniles, shoplifting, or vandalism usually round out the list of officers' least-favorite police reports to take and write. Again, the sense of accomplishment, closure, and efficient use of the officers' time come into play.

Burglary reports, those with very little physical evidence, no suspect information, or no other viable clues or leads are often little better than the paper they're written on. Most people have no idea of the brand names, model numbers, or even colors for their stolen TVs, VCRs, and other appliances. Stolen jewelry, cash, silverware, etc. are usually hard to trace, identify, or recover.

Traffic collisions present a variety of other problems for officers arriving on the scene. The participants are usually mad at one another; the physical evidence is nearly always moved before the officers can look at it; and each party tells a different story about the course of events. Witnesses are sometimes reluctant to get involved, or worse, tell the officers what they heard instead of what they actually saw.

Many officers dislike taking traffic collision reports because in most cities these reports require them to gather more information than any other report. There are a myriad of boxes to be checked, names to be entered, insurance policy numbers, witness information, diagrams, injuries, and property damage to document, and statements to take. Even the smallest fender-bender report can take an inordinate amount of time to complete.

Non-injury hit-and-run reports are another unpopular police report. These cases typically involve supermarket parking lot swideswipes, shopping mall parking lot door bangs, and late-night residential street body crunches. In each example, the officers have little to go on except for the physical evidence in front of them. With no eyewitnesses, an inexact time frame of several hours or even days, and no description of the other car except maybe the color, these cases are difficult to solve and even harder to prosecute.

City attorneys will secretly admit that because their offices are usually short-staffed and swamped with more serious cases, they won't even attempt to prosecute hit-and-run cases with no injuries. Officers dislike these cases from a report standpoint because they are usually required to complete two separate reports: one traffic collision report and one hit-and-run vehicle report. Since these accidents happen predominantly on private property, like parking lots and driveways, it's often difficult to take measurements and to draw an accurate diagram of the scene. Coupled with the rare chance of catching the suspect or locating his or her car, it's no wonder these reports are frustrating.

But since nearly all insurance companies require some police report of the damage before they pay a claim, these reports are a necessity for the victim. Most police agencies realize this and will complete hit-and-run reports as a courtesy to the public.

While most officers take satisfaction in arresting adult offenders and filling out the arrest forms, juvenile arrest cases are a completely different and more complex matter. In most minor juvenile cases (and in some overcrowded cities, major cases) the arresting officer must complete the report and then turn the offending juvenile over to his or her parents. Only rarely do juveniles go to a juvenile correctional center for admission. Usually the parents must come from home to the police station to get their son or daughter. As many juvenile arrests happen at night (vandalism, car theft, car burglaries, curfew violations, drinking, etc.), officers don't like having to rouse sleepy parents from bed and then wait around for them to get to the station. Mix this long waiting and processing time with an uncooperative, unremorseful, or even hostile teenager, and you can understand why many officers dislike juvenile contact reports.

Rounding out the list of unpopular police reports are shoplifting and petty theft from drug and clothing stores. These cases nearly always involve juveniles which, as we have discovered, means the officer must wait for parents to arrive to take custody of their child. Further, most officers don't like having to complete a two-page crime case (for the crime of petty theft) and a four-page arrest report (for the shoplifter) for a case that the store will rarely prosecute. Most stores hit with these "shrinkage" cases merely ask for restitution for the goods and warn the thief never to enter the store again. This appearance of a "slap on the wrist" coupled with two hours of report writing only serves to anger most officers.

We know that most officers do not mind writing arrest reports because they can see their work come full circle; and we know that they don't like to write certain "go nowhere" reports. One thing, however, is clear: police officers will take all reports when asked to by the public. The ability to put his or her true feelings aside is the hallmark of a good officer. Most officers will take a report, if the facts and the environment warrant one, without regard to how they really feel about the case. They realize that a police report is valuable because it serves to document an incident, and it may be important later.

However, some less conscientious officers tend to believe that once a report leaves their ink-stained fingers they don't have to think about it again unless the case goes to court, and they don't give the report the attention it deserves. They forget what happens down the line once their paperwork gets to the Records Division, and they don't really care.

What these officers fail to appreciate is that there are many people whose careers relate indirectly to law enforcement. While these people don't wear badges, their work depends a great deal on the quality (and quantity) of police reports. In no case is this involvement more evident than with traffic accidents.

The Importance of Traffic Collision Reports

The list of interested parties—not just Driver One and Driver Two—includes insurance claims adjusters, accident investigators and reconstructionists, plaintiff and defense attorneys, paralegals, body shop owners, expert witnesses, medical doctors, and chiropractors.

Some officers have an attitude that says, "Who cares? I just write the accident report. After I do the investigation, I just ship it over to Records and let them sort it out."

Part of that is true, but the ramifications of the investigation in a typical traffic collision case go far beyond just two cars involved in a crash. There are many reasons why traffic collision reports are so time-consuming and full of what seems like minute detail. Most of those reasons revolve around civil liability issues and city, state, and federal governmental record-keeping requirements.

Most cities have a traffic engineering department ranging in size from one full-time employee to several hundred. One of the main reasons this unit even exists is to document the number, location, and type of automobile accidents in the city. Two hundred accidents per year may not be too high for a bustling, mid-size city, but if 30 percent of those accidents happen at one intersection, then the potential for expensive lawsuits becomes a real issue. Consequently, municipalities rely on their police and sheriff's departments to document car accidents and help highlight any significant problem areas.

Similarly, each state has its own traffic accident documentation needs. Various state agencies relating to transportation safety keep track of accidents by city, county, region, and population. This affects long-range planning, state highway patrol manpower allocations, traffic safety standards, construction funding, and a host of other issues.

Lastly, all this information meanders its way through various bureaucracies until it reaches the federal level. Agencies like the Department of Transportation and the National Transportation Safety Board take a keen interest in city and state accident figures. This information is used to create accident prevention programs, federal safety guidelines for automobile manufacturers, and federal spending plans for cities, counties, and states.

Besides the impact upon transportation, safety, and planning agencies, traffic accidents usually involve injured people who call upon attorneys to settle their roadway differences. The information or lack thereof on a traffic collision report may mean the difference between a lifetime of uncompensated pain and suffering for an injured party or a huge insurance settlement for that person.

Attorneys rely on police report information as their "eyes and ears" at the scene of an accident. Sketchy, incomplete reports can hurt accident victims. Poor reports can open the municipality to liability and may even expose the officer to a civil damages claim.

A thorough police report, which includes the physical evidence, the insurance information, and the witnesses names, addresses, and phone numbers, can give enough information to make all parties in the case happy.

A police officer can develop a good reputation among supervisors and prosecutors as a skilled report writer. Likewise, personal injury or criminal defense attorneys become familiar with police reports and know who writes a good one and who does not. The knowledge of who wrote the report can influence their overall approach to the case. Good reports are harder to impeach than bad ones. Unfortunately, some officers and some police agencies don't put much effort into good report writing skills. Because report writing lacks that certain glamor appeal, it often gets short shrift in terms of academy training and advanced officer in-service training.

At a typical car accident scene, even veteran officers have a tendency to let some seemingly less important information fall through the cracks as they try to get everything done. An officer working a crash alone may have to direct traffic, order tow trucks, assist the injured, and interview witnesses. It's hard to remember to do everything, especially during the stress of a car crash situation.

Police Reports and Attorneys

Officers can also neglect many important details while completing crime case and arrest reports. Faced with time pressures (like wanting to get off work on time or no overtime budget in their city) or hostile or uncooperative victims, witnesses, and suspects, officers may take shortcuts to save time and energy. These shortcuts may seem innocuous at first, but they can come back to haunt the officer weeks, months, or even years later in court.

Attorneys and their paralegals face a double-edged sword when it comes to the accuracy of police reports. Clearly, all those living in a community protected by police want safer streets, less crime, and a careful, humane, and aggressive police department to look after them. Yet, personal injury attorneys and criminal defense specialists make their livings reading, interpreting, and analyzing police reports for their clients. And they aren't reading these reports because they particularly enjoy them, but because they are looking for mistakes and errors of commission or omission that will help their clients and thereby earn their fees.

Few attorneys truly enjoy attacking police reports for errors, but it comes with the territory. The nature of practicing certain types of law calls for a careful examination of these official documents because, in many cases, they offer the only description of what actually happened at an accident scene, in a crime case, or at an arrest scene.

Personal injury auto accident attorneys look for mistakes relating to the officer's examination of the accident scene: his or her opinion of the primary cause; errors made about the physical evidence; incorrect witness statements; errors concerning related factors like the sobriety of the drivers, witnesses, or passengers; the position, location, and veracity of the witnesses; mistakes made in the scale diagram, etc.

Criminal defense attorneys read police arrest reports with an equally careful eye, looking for: points of error relating to probable cause; illegal search and seizure; illegal interrogations; damaged or illegally obtained evidence; and any other supposed flaw in the officer's arrest procedure in relation to a point of law that could offer a chance of acquittal for their clients. This careful scrutiny is just part of the job of being a lawyer. It is an exacting, important task often entrusted to a careful, thorough paralegal.

Getting Police Reports

Rare is the client who brings his or her police report to the initial attorneys' meeting. Most clients have no idea how to get a police report or, in some startling cases, even how to find the police station. A prospective client may also have no access to his or her police report because of time delays at the police agency. In many law enforcement departments, reports written on the day of the accident or arrest may not reach the Records Division for several days and won't be available to the participants until seven to 10 working days later, and then only between certain working hours on specified days of the week.

A report release waiver should always be a part of each "new client" file folder package. After the client signs this release form, make at least three or four extra copies for the file. These waivers are useful and may be mandatory in many states in order for you to get access to police, medical, and insurance records. Most of these agencies have strict rules that go with even stricter state and federal privacy of information laws. No release usually means no report.

Actually getting a copy of the client's police report can often be an exercise in supreme patience. Usually the job falls to the paralegal in a small law office or the designated "errand person" in a larger firm. If the task falls to you and you've been having some difficulty getting access to police reports, try the following steps to ease your way:

1. *Make sure you have a signed and complete records release from the client.*

2. *Locate the report before you do anything.* This is usually easier said than done. In some small counties, the sheriff's department serves certain areas and the police department serves the rest. However, inside a large county the sheriff will serve the outlying areas (and run the jails), and several different, smaller police departments will serve their respective cities within the county. In an area the size of Los Angeles County, for example, you may have over 100 different law enforcement agencies besides the Los Angeles Police Department and the Los Angeles Sheriff's Department.

   If you work in a multi-city community, like Los Angeles, San Diego, New York, New Jersey, Dallas-Fort Worth, or the Washington, DC, area, it's imperative that you pinpoint the exact location of the client's accident or arrest. Ask him or her what specific agency responded to the scene and who might have taken the report. Don't forget that the State Highway Patrol may also have jurisdiction. In some large-scale car crashes or multi-jurisdictional arrests, the client may not know exactly who took the report.

   In other cases, the client may have been injured so severely that he or she has no memory of the incident except that it happened. If you're not sure of the location, get a map and verify the street location. Either way, if you know which agency took the report, you can save yourself much time, gasoline, and shoe leather.

3. *Call the police agency, ask for the Records Division, and have the client's last name, incident date, and type of incident ready to give to the clerk.* Keep in mind that people in the Records Division are typically overworked and underpaid, doing a tedious, high-volume job. Be as polite and friendly as you can. Even the smallest human touch (a joke about the

weather or the workload) can mean the difference between an "I can't find your report and I'm too busy to look" and "Let me look a little harder for you." Making friends with these clerks is not a bad idea, especially if you expect to deal with them frequently for your report needs. Better to have a bureaucrat on your side than against you or merely indifferent.

4. *When you give the client's information, be prepared to write down the case number.* This will speed things when you go to pick up the report. Ask how much the report will cost. Some agencies charge by the page (typically $1 per sheet), and others charge by the report. Ask if any photos came with the report and how much these will cost. Many local and state police agencies will take accident-scene photos in death or serious-injury car accident cases.

5. *If you're not sure, ask the clerk for the hours of operation at the Records Division.* Make sure you bring the client's release and a blank check to pay for the report. By filling in the check at the counter, you avoid problems related to page miscount or improper calculations of the fee.

6. *When you get the report and before you leave, read it over quickly to be sure it's the correct one.* Make sure the copy is clear and legible and you can read every page. Check to see if the pages are in order and none are missing. Don't hesitate to ask for new copies if the report is fuzzy or incomplete.

7. *Plan your visits carefully.* The best times to go to Records are bright and early in the morning or during the hours between 1:30 and 3:00 p.m. Most people (paralegals included) try to go on their lunch hours, and this can mean a long and agonizing wait. If you have more than one case, try to get all the reports you need during one visit. If you call first, get the report numbers, and arrive at a strategic time of the day with the appropriate releases and checks, you should have few problems getting what you need.

Reading Police Reports

Just as there are good, best-selling books and poor, just-sit-there books, there are good and poor police reports. Good ones are written by officers who have realized early on that the path to promotion starts with good people skills and with better-than-most report-writing skills. Furthermore, these officers have also discovered, possibly through hard experience, that good police reports can prevent nasty civil suits. In an era in which armed robbers can successfully sue officers for injuries they received during gun battles, this is no small factor.

I recall reviewing a traffic collision report written by an El Cajon, California, police traffic officer. The nighttime accident involved a man riding a bicycle and the driver of a passenger car. The resulting crash between small bike and large car cost the rider his life.

In the ensuing investigation at the scene, the traffic officer was able to prove the bicycle rider was completely at fault. The next day, aided by the San Diego County Sheriff's helicopter, the officer flew over the accident scene and took many aerial photos to include in his report. This thorough officer knew his job: document the scene completely and let the physical evidence tell the report reader what actually happened.

In preparing another traffic report, this same officer impounded one of the cars involved in the crash, took it to a certified traffic collision expert mechanic and had him analyze the entire car. From this careful scrutiny, the officer showed that the car did have its headlights on at the time of the crash. The mechanic's report even went so far as to measure the amount of brake fluid in the car's brake cylinder reservoir.

While some jaded traffic investigators may say that this amount of work is excessive, I say this officer should get high praise for doing his job to the utmost. His attention to detail as well as his ability to show the "big picture" has probably saved his municipality, his police department, and himself from even the hint of a lawsuit by any traffic accident participant. His devotion to duty means that, like it or not, all parties involved in these traffic crashes got a full and complete report of what happened and why.

While traffic investigation officers like this one do exist, they are sadly the exception rather than the rule. The majority of officers in this country can produce an adequate police report, but few are willing to go the extra mile necessary to complete a truly sterling piece of work. Time deadlines, other cases, and pressures from peers or supervisors can prevent an otherwise good officer from writing the best police report he or she can.

Here is a somewhat alarming paradox: mediocre police reports that leave out the facts and expose law enforcement agencies and their municipalities to civil suits can become your "trump card" in a traffic accident or criminal defense case. Since many police reports are merely adequate, i.e., "I came, I saw, I wrote, I left," you can learn to read reports involving your clients with a more practiced, if not jaundiced, eye.

Finding errors, exploiting omissions, or attacking the officer's experience or training may not sound too friendly nor make you popular with the police, but it does offer one time-honored way for attorneys to win cases for their clients. The more you know about how certain police officers write their reports, the better chance you have to exploit a possible weakness to your advantage.

With few exceptions, the two kinds of police reports that would most affect the general practice, personal injury, or criminal defense law firm where you work are those involving traffic collisions and those involving arrests.

It's not safe or accurate to generalize about what police reports actually say or look like because each police agency (local, state, military, or federal) uses its own forms. What works for one won't work for the other. Police reports may be standardized statewide, countywide, or not at all. An agency may copy an adjoining department's report forms or use something completely different. But while each agency may use different forms, we can make certain assumptions based on the fact that, in the end, all reports will cover the same topics.

Most police activities fall into two categories: reactive and proactive. In reactive situations, officers come across incidents of crime or criminals and deal with them accordingly. This includes their response to radio calls, to citizens who flag them down while driving through their beat, and finally, to things they themselves notice as they patrol.

In car accident cases, the officers may be sent to the site at the request of the dispatcher; they may be told of the crash by a passerby; or they may in fact witness or drive past the accident themselves. As a side note, if your client was involved in an accident witnessed by the police and he or she is at fault, don't expect the report to be much help for your cause.

Arrest cases are similar to car accidents. Officers may get a radio call which leads them to arrest someone; they may be told of some criminal activity going on, e.g., a burglary, a fight, car tampering, etc.; or they may come across someone they see committing a crime. They may even spot a known fugitive.

While these reactive instances cause officers to take action when they learn of problems, proactive police work is entirely different. Reactive police activities make up the bulk of police work. Proactive policing, though not as common, often leads to more spectacular results. In these cases, officers will go to high-crime areas and wait for things to happen. Narcotics, robbery, and burglary stakeouts are examples; undercover, wiretapping, and infiltration operations are others. Here, the police are ready and willing to take on criminals by setting traps for them. Most proactive police work that doesn't involve special uniformed street patrols is conducted by experienced detectives and other veteran police investigators.

Another example of proactive policing involving traffic matters is the use of radar guns and so-called speed traps in certain heavily-traveled and high-accident areas. Here, the police are attempting to solve a problem using a proactive approach.

What does all this mean to you as a report reader? It should help you understand the hows and whys of your client's involvement with the police, as an accident victim, as an arrestee, and as a citizen of the community.

Many personal injury attorneys focus their practice on traffic-related matters—minor or major injury car accidents, hit-and-run cases with injury, wrongful deaths, or fatal accidents. If you work for a personal injury attorney, you can expect to spend much of your time reviewing the police reports that correspond to these events.

And since criminal defense attorneys focus their efforts on clients involved in Driving Under the Influence cases, narcotics arrests, and felony or certain misdemeanor cases, you, as a paralegal to a criminal defense .attorney, will tend to read many police arrest reports related to these matters.

Have no fear—report reading experience comes with time. You may know nothing about police reports and the associated jargon and terminology, or you may be an old pro, with enough knowledge to teach an Academy class on the subject of police reports. Either way, you should realize that the forms for police reports are in a constant state of flux. Department administrators are often inveterate tinkerers, and they don't feel satisfied unless they're changing police reports to meet new or supposedly new needs. One southern California police department changed its arrestee information sheet three times in six months. Police officers had to learn to fill out each one, and paralegals had to learn to read them.

This should warn you to be alert for new versions and new layouts of the same old reports. The forms may change colors or the number of little boxes to be checked may grow from five to fifty, but one thing will not change—the language.

In any client case, traffic or arrest, the key to understanding the police report lies in the narrative, or what the officer writes as an explanation for his or her actions and the actions of the other case participants at the scene. Depending on the police agency, the report you read could be chock-full of jargon and inside terminology that only other police officers (or somewhat confused prosecutors) could understand, or it could be written in plain English, with a minimum of police-related terminology.

Many police departments go to great lengths to train and retrain their officers to write in plain English. Their goal is to avoid written statements like, "The violator's vehicle faced in a westerly direction after it struck the parked vehicle" or "The suspect was searched and a gun was removed." The first statement sounds as if it were written by a computer and not a human, and the second, passive voice example doesn't say who exactly searched the suspect or where exactly the gun was found.

A clearer way to make the first statement might be: "After hitting the parked car, the vehicle came to rest facing west." And for the second example, the sentence "Officer Davis searched the suspect and removed a gun from his right front jacket pocket" might tell the story better.

As you review traffic accident reports, focus your attention on three specific areas: the client, defendant, and witness information; the primary cause; and the facts surrounding the accident. You'll use the first part to complete the client's case file (names, addresses, phone numbers, insurance policy information, etc.) and the second and third to look for statements, evidence, or errors in your client's favor.

The most important piece of information on a traffic collision report (besides the other party's insurance policy number) is the determination of fault or the Primary Cause Factor (PCF). If the defendant was at fault, you have a good chance of winning the case based solely on the validity of the report, the credibility of the client, and the availability of any witnesses.

If the client appears at fault, you have to ask yourself if this determination could be subject to a legitimate argument that might change this outcome. If the report is in error or if you can find a witness who tells a completely different story, then you might have a chance with the case.

Why only a chance? Because to many insurance adjusters, judges, or arbitrators, police reports are worth their weight in gold. Many of these people will admit, "If that's the way the officer says it happened, then I tend to believe the officer."

Do police officers make mistakes when they complete traffic collision reports? Yes, occasionally they do. So why do these reports get such a high regard? Because the people who settle car accident cases tend to think that the officer is primarily an impartial observer, paid to weigh the facts, statements, and evidence fairly, and render a decision about the fault without regard to any biases. For the most part this is true. Police officers are trained in traffic matters to analyze the skid marks, vehicle damage, and other physical evidence, weigh it with the statements made by the drivers and any witnesses, and add in their training, experience, and knowledge of the area to make their decisions.

With your knowledge of how adjusters and judges weigh police reports, does this mean that you should suggest to your attorney that he or she drop the case because the report favors the other side? Sometimes the answer should be a firm and confident "yes." There is little sense clinging to false hopes with a case that is clearly a loser for your firm.

Still, before you suggest this drastic alternative, do a little digging and look below the surface of the report. Police officers are just as human as everyone else. They are subject to the same biases, prejudices, and preconceived opinions as the rest of us. Consider the following scenarios before you decide that a traffic case is a certain "dumper":

- The client speaks broken English, has a very shy personality (especially toward uniformed authority figures), and did not get the opportunity to explain his version of the events to the officer. Here, the other driver's stronger (English) voice and more dominant personality may have influenced the officer into believing only one side of the story.

- The client was severely injured at the scene, knocked unconscious, and taken away in an ambulance. With no witnesses and no passengers to offer another version, the officer spoke only to the other driver to get the story.

- The client is an anti-police person. His or her demeanor with the officers at the scene was clearly hostile, argumentative, and maybe even combative. The other driver, on the other hand, is a nice sweet old lady who reminded the reporting officer of his kindly grandmother.

See the biases and preconceived opinions in each case? While it's still possible that your client may indeed be at fault in each scenario, the chances are good that certain outside factors may have influenced the officer's opinions and caused him or her to believe the other party.

Without the benefit of having witnessed the accident, or interviewed an independent eyewitness who saw it, the officer is forced to rely on other considerations such as the physical evidence. If there is little evidence or the officer is untrained in recognizing its importance, your client may bear the brunt of his or her own circumstances, like the inability to speak clear English, severe injuries, or a hostile demeanor.

Since the first step in any case is to talk with the client, try to get a complete picture of the events that took place. Some of the circumstances surrounding the accident may bring other issues like those above to light.

Traffic Collision Reports: Understanding the Jargon

Some career fields tend to be a bit heavy on jargon—computer science, engineering, insurance, and banking come to mind. Police work is no exception; it clearly ranks among the jargon-rich professions, behind only, perhaps, the military and the federal government. Police traffic collision reports attempt to tell the readers, and in most cases there are many of them, who was driving where and who crashed into whom. This sounds simple on the surface, but with acres of jargon filling the pages, it can be a challenge to discover this information without a qualified "police-speak" interpreter.

Keep in mind that, in most instances, the only agency that uses the same traffic collision report for all its officers is the State Highway Patrol. At least you have some clarity here because officers from all over the state use the same form. To complicate things even more, some police and sheriff's agencies use the State Highway Patrol form for their reports, while others use their own (usually a conglomeration of the Highway Patrol version mixed in with regional information).

In nearly all traffic collision reports, the officers will refer to the participants in one of three ways:

1. P-1, P-2, etc. for Party One or Participant One, etc.

2. D-1, D-2, etc. for Driver One, Driver Two, etc.

3. V-1, V-2, etc. for Vehicle One, Vehicle Two, etc.

If this isn't complicated enough, keep in mind that in some reports, P-1 (or D-1 or V-1) is always listed at fault, and in others, P-2 (or D-2 or V-2) is always listed as the at-fault driver. How do you know from agency to agency and report to report? You must read the narrative to see who did what to whom and how the officer refers to the party at fault.

Other common abbreviations include:

- ICP—Initial Contact Point; refers to the actual physical street measurement (usually in feet or tenths of a mile) where one car collided with another.

- POI—Point of Impact; another way to refer to the ICP.

- POR—Point of Rest; indicates how far a vehicle or a body (in fatal accidents) traveled after the initial ICP/POI. A long distance may indicate a vehicle's high rate of speed.

- PCF—The Primary Collision Factor; tells you why the accident happened (in the opinion of the investigating officer), e.g., Following Too Close, Speed Unsafe For Conditions, Unsafe Movement to the Left or Right, Violation of Right of Way, Illegal U-Turn, etc.

- C.O.P.—Complaint of Pain; tells you who was injured and how severely.

- W-1, E-1, S-1, N-1, etc.; shorthand for the first Westbound, Eastbound, Southbound, or Northbound lane (as you count left to right from the center divider). The lane to the right of the "one" lane would be the "two" lane, etc. Freeways would count from the one or "fast" lane all the way left to right to the "four" or "slow" lane.

- wb, eb, sb, nb; another way to abbreviate westbound, eastbound, etc.

- wcl, ecl, scl, ncl; west curbline, east curbline, south curbline, and north curbline.

Traffic investigators use feet and specific curblines to pinpoint the exact location of the accident. An accident in an intersection may have occurred "25 feet north of the south curbline of Maple Street and 18 feet east of the west curbline of Ash Street." This allows other reviewing parties like traffic investigators, insurance adjusters, city claims personnel, etc., to pinpoint the location of the crash.

Most traffic collisions will also have a diagram, and these vary in quality from excellent to dismal depending on the drawing skills of the reporting officer. The size, complexity, and accuracy of the diagram may be determined by the severity of the injuries in the case. In most midsize to large cities, serious injury and fatal traffic accidents are handled by specially trained uniformed traffic accident investigators. These officers will have gone through a special 40-hour "Skid School" to learn about skid patterns, braking distances, collision damage, and how to investigate and document serious collisions.

If your client was involved in any part of a serious or fatal accident, the report will be much more detailed than a simple rear-end crash or a similar minor injury accident. The diagram will be of full-page size and will include specific measurements and the location of all evidence, including vehicles, obstructions, pedestrians, witnesses, etc.

Since these serious accident reports are usually completed by well-trained accident investigators with many years of police traffic service, they are more difficult to dispute than other less complex reports. However, many law firms handling serious injury (and big-money) cases will hire private traffic accident reconstructionists to review the report and compare it with their own interpretation of the crash scene. If the police report and the private consultant's report differ greatly, the matter will probably end up in court.

Many of these expert traffic reconstructionists are also ex–police officers with a significant background in traffic accident reporting. We'll discuss the best way to use these types of experts in the next chapter.

As you look at a typical traffic collision report, keep a few other important factors and questions in mind:

- Most traffic diagrams are written so that the North position points up on the page.

- Does the report contain an accurate diagram? Do the lane measurements appear correct or do they look like rough guesses? Most officers pace off the lane widths and other numbers like the POI and POR. These figures can vary widely in their accuracy and may have a significant impact upon the outcome of the case.

- Are there any street conditions that bear noting? This may include the presence (or lack) of city barricades to cover a huge hole or ongoing construction; flag personnel who should have controlled a dangerous intersection; any unusual road problems like spilled gasoline, oil, water, sand, or gravel that may have caused drivers to react in other than normal ways.

- Were the electronic traffic control signals working correctly at the time of the collision? Were city or state construction crews present, and did they see or cause the crash? Is there a chance to prove city or state liability?

- Are there any discrepancies about who owns or insures the car? Is there any question of negligent entrustment with the defendant's car?

- Are the ambulance and hospital personnel properly listed? Does the report indicate the police, fire, ambulance, and other medical personnel who may have responded? You may need to subpoena these people later.

- Have you or your client remembered to notify the State Department of Motor Vehicles about the accident? Failure to do so could bring the client a nasty license suspension notice.

If you work for a law firm that does any personal injury work at all, police traffic collision reports should be your bread and butter. Thorough reports can help you win most car accident cases. If the reports are good and in your client's favor, use them to your advantage. If the reports are poor, filled with errors, or not in your client's favor, exploit the errors to your benefit or work to get them changed. We'll discuss the procedures for amending a police report in the next chapter.

Reading Arrest Reports

While traffic collision reports tend to contain mostly factual data, police arrest reports tend to rely more on the officer's observations, opinions, and his or her interpretation of the events leading up to the arrest. As such, there is obviously much more room for discussion and impeachment. True, some cases are clearly open and shut, or "slam dunks" as cops like to call them. Here, the best any defense attorney can hope for is for some fair treatment at the plea bargain conference. But many cases do offer some ambiguity. These cases demand careful scrutiny of the arrest reports so that the attorney can prepare an effective defense.

Arrest reports vary in detail and length from agency to agency. As a reviewer, you should focus your attention on the narrative since this represents the "meat and potatoes" of any arrest report. Here's how a typical arrest report will break down into narrative sections:

Charges: This section will tell you what the client was charged with, including the specific code section and enabling code book, e.g., the Penal Code, the Vehicle Code, the Health and Safety Code, etc.

Origin/probable cause: This section gives you two important sets of facts: how the officer came to notice the arrestee (radio call, routine observations, a tip) and what led the officer to stop and detain the person (weaving while driving, bizarre behavior, running from a ringing alarm while carrying a VCR). This is the most delicate part of the report because much of the rest of the case (searches, arrest, etc.) hinges on good and legal probable cause. Read very carefully here, highlighting with a pen the areas that may be inconsistent with case law.

Officer actions: This section explains what actions the officer took to apprehend the person and why he or she took those actions. It includes things the officer may have seen or heard that led him or her to make an arrest.

Victim/witness statements: These are descriptive statements based on comments the officer has solicited from crime victims and nearby witnesses. These statements are typically written in a looser, paraphrased style: "The witness told me in essence that he was sitting on the bus bench when he saw the suspect run up and knock the victim to the ground. . . ."

Suspect statements: These are almost always verbatim, quoted statements made by the arrestee, either after the Miranda admonition or spontaneously before Miranda warnings. Officers will usually document these statements as quoted passages (Officer: "Then what did you do?" Suspect: "I put the gun in my jacket pocket. . . ."). Remember, police officers have been taught to interview victims and witnesses and to interrogate suspects. The report should reflect a professional approach to taking statements.

Evidence: This section consists of an inventory of any evidence recovered at the scene or taken from the suspect and the information as to the disposition of the evidence: "One small plastic baggie of marijuana, removed from the suspect's right front pants pocket. Impounded at the station on Tag #1234."

Injuries/damage: This section includes any description of injuries that the victim or suspect may have sustained or any damage to property caused by the crime.

With any criminal defense matter, keep the client's own statement of the facts in mind. What did he or she tell you or the attorney handling the case at the initial meeting? How does this compare with the officer's version? What discrepancies do you see in either story? Are there any obvious mistakes in the report in terms of case law, illegal detention, or unlawful search and seizure?

Rock-solid arrest reports are hard to beat. Good officers know from training and long years of experience just what to put in the report to "sell" the report to their supervisors and to the prosecuting city and district attorneys who will read it later. But even the best officers will take shortcuts, leave out pertinent information, or fail to explain their actions sufficiently to get a conviction. In a traffic collision or criminal defense case, the police report, the information you get from the client, and witness statements may be all you have to go on. If it's possible to win the case, you'll find the ammunition you need to help you right there in the report.

four

USING OTHER PROFESSIONALS: Working with the Police and Civilian Investigators, Process Servers, Adjusters, and Other Experts

"My idea of the ideal jury is twelve Irish unionists deciding the case of my client, Patrick O'Brien, a union bricklayer, who was run over by Chauncy Marlborough's Rolls-Royce while Marlborough was on his way to deposit $50,000 in the bank."—Melvin Belli

F act: Most police officers don't like attorneys! Fact: Many attorneys don't think much of the police profession either! Surprised? Probably not. A relationship tenuous from the start has gradually deteriorated with repeated unsatisfactory contacts. Excessive media coverage of high-profile criminal trials often puts police officers in a bad light. And previous unpleasant courtroom encounters lead many police officers to dislike attorneys and to resist dealing with them if at all possible.

Similarly, some attorneys have a noticeable tendency to look down upon the law enforcement profession as being too aggressive, biased, judgmental, and ham-handed with its cases. They also tend to see the police officer as primarily a blue-collar worker bent on issuing heavy doses of street justice or locked into a totally inflexible position that doesn't consider the needs of the community.

In either case, lawyer jokes and cop jokes abound on both sides, and each appears to treat the other the same way a cobra treats a mongoose—very carefully.

All this animosity, justified or not, can put you in a precarious position as a paralegal. If your law firm has any dealings with the police or with police-related matters, e.g., clients in traffic collisions or criminal defense cases, you can find a number of figurative and literal barriers in your path.

As we discussed in the previous chapter, just getting a copy of a police report can turn into an all-day affair. Police agencies, as with most bureaucracies, are stifled by rules and regulations that interfere with their ability to help the public. As the old sage Will Rogers so eloquently put it, "The last thing a public servant wants to do is serve the public."

You may have a tough time locating a specific report, but that effort pales in comparison with the assignment of getting any help, new information, or even a return phone call from a detective about your case. This task can be an entirely different exercise in futility. If you're the one asked to track down information from police officials, better put a seatbelt around your desk; it can be a bumpy ride.

Police professionals tend to see lawyers as people who only come around to undo the good things the police have done. Lawyers capitalize on seemingly small technicalities in the law to free known criminals from jail, sue officers and their departments for superfluous civil cases, point out report-writing errors and magnify them to the nth degree with judges and juries, and finally, embarrass or humiliate officers on the witness stand.

Many officers have learned painful lessons from criminal defense attorneys and civil litigation attorneys who have "barbecued" them for their errors. The officers have long memories about who reddened their cheeks in the courtroom. From the first day of the police academy and throughout their careers, the police are taught to speak carefully around attorneys or risk looking like fools in front of the public and their courthouse peers. These lessons run deep and probably do much to interfere with the flow of information between attorneys and the police. Most officers have clear memories of courtroom encounters that made the minutes tick by like days. Whereas many defense and civil litigation attorneys consider their treatment of police officers as just another part of the job, the officers themselves can recount each encounter verbatim.

This "enemy camps" mentality only gets in your way. Unfortunately, years of historical animosity precede you. Keep this story in mind whenever you prepare to deal with police officials: One of the largest police training companies in the country offers a three-day police officer survival seminar. This program appears in various large cities and is well-attended by officers looking for new tactics. Besides the usual collection of police books, video tapes, and sports clothes, the firm sells a t-shirt with Shakespeare's well-quoted line, "The first thing we do, let's kill all the lawyers." Do you doubt that this t-shirt sells like hotcakes to the officers in attendance? Forewarned is forearmed.

Making Contact

Getting through to a selected police officer can be easy, moderately difficult, or next to impossible. Just calling up the police station, leaving your name, law firm name, and telephone number, probably won't help much.

Since most officers still remember their last painful run-in with an attorney (either professionally or personally, as in a nasty divorce case), they can rarely think of any reason to go out of their way to help an attorney or paralegal who calls them for assistance.

To help you locate an individual officer, consider the following checklist of questions:

1. *What is the officer's full name and ID number?* A large police agency can have three or four R. Garcias, D. Smiths, or M. Washingtons. Look at the bottom of the report for the officer's ID number (it's not usually his or her badge number, but an identifying number that stays for the entire career).

2. *Where and for whom does the officer work?* As we discussed in the chapter on locating police reports, you need to know where the officer works to find him or her. Some cities have several different substations, precincts, or divisions. Armed with a name and ID number, you can call the agency's Personnel Division and

explain that you're trying to find the officer. The Personnel Division may send you in the right direction.

3. *What shift hours does the officer work?* Some police reports will give this information at the bottom, near the officer's name, e.g., W-1, E-2, or N-3. These mean that the officer works at the Western Division station (first watch, or "day shift" hours), at the Eastern Division station (second watch, or "swing shift" hours), or at the Northern Division station (third watch, or the "graveyard" shift overnight hours). Or you may see "1, 2, or 3" or "A, B, or C" to indicate first, second, or third shift.

   Finally, you can look at the time the report was written for one last clue to the officer's working hours. Reports taken at 11:00 a.m. indicate a day shift; 6:00 p.m. indicates a swing shift; and reports penned at 4:30 a.m. indicate a graveyard shift. This time reference doesn't appear on all reports, but it may give you a window of opportunity to help you reach the officer.

   Knowing when a patrol officer works can help you plan your calls to arrive before he or she goes into the field or at the close or start of your business day.

4. *What are the officer's days off?* Knowing this valuable information can help you plan your calls much more effectively. Calling for officers on Monday, Tuesday, and Wednesday when they are off will only irritate the message takers (usually other officers or overworked secretaries) and cause you to look unprofessional. Papering their mailboxes with pink return-call slips may even be counterproductive.

   Some officers work five eight-hour days with two days off, while others may work four 10-hour days with three days off. Find out when it's best to call for the officer, and schedule your phone time to increase your chances of reaching him or her.

5. *What is the officer's job title or rank?* Most crime case, arrest, and injury/death traffic collision reports are originally taken

by patrol officers and later handled by detectives. For error corrections, you'll want to speak to the patrol officer who took the case. For case updates or other significant information about your client, you'll usually want to speak with the detective assigned. In some cities, the detectives are assigned to area stations and work on everything that happens in that area. In others, they work on only one type of crime, e.g., burglaries, robberies, narcotics, etc. Finding the appropriate detective is usually harder than locating the originating patrol officers, but in most cases, the detective will be in more of a position to give you help or information.

6. *Are other officers named on the report? Will you need to talk to them?* If so, consider leaving messages for each and improving your odds that one or more will return your call.

    The best way to leave a message for an officer is to give only your first and last name and phone number. If you have a direct phone line right to your desk, so much the better. Leaving a message with the name of a law firm on it is a sure way to help your message slip hit the wastebasket. Remember, as noble as your client's case may be, and as right as you think you are, helping attorneys make money is not very important to the police. Be subtle and just leave your name, number, and the best time to call.

So what happens when you actually reach these officers at their station or they return your call? Kill them with kindness. Overwhelm them with your politeness. Startle them with your professionalism and courtesy.

Imagine what typically races through an officer's mind when he or she receives the following phone call: "Officer Johnson, this is paralegal Smith from the law office of Jones, Jones, and Jones. . . ."

Immediately, two things spring into the officer's mental frame: "What do THEY want? What, if anything, have I done wrong?" Imagine how you would respond if those two items were first and foremost in your mind. Suspicion, hostility, and wariness become the officer's watchwords. Meet these barriers head-on by being as friendly, open, and professional as possible, but don't beat around the bush or keep these officers guessing what you called about. Tell them the client's name, ask if they recall the case, and ask if they have time to speak with you about the matter.

Be aware of police department protocol when you speak to officers. Most agencies do not allow their officers to comment on pending criminal cases or arrest reports, especially those that are still in the investigation stage. Furthermore, most officers will not answer any questions about cases or reports awaiting trial. These inquiries must go through the appropriate city or district attorney. Don't expect much help if you fail to go through the appropriate channels.

But while most officers will not speak openly about criminal cases, traffic collisions are a completely different story. In these matters, the majority of police officers will be happy to speak to you about their view of the case. Since officers know most of these matters are handled civilly, without a court trial, they are less cautious with their opinions. They may answer your telephone queries with complete disclosure or they may simply say, "If you want to know what happened, review my report, and if necessary, I'll testify at a deposition or hearing, but you'll have to pay my department for my time."

In either case, thank the officer for his or her time and continue to be as professional as possible, even if you didn't solve your immediate concerns. There are other ways to get information.

Correcting Report Errors

In most traffic collision cases, you'll want to clarify portions of the officer's report (witness statements, directions, road conditions, etc.), ask more questions about certain issues (vehicle damage, injuries, etc.), and/or correct any obvious errors in the report. While the first two matters may go without a hitch, the last one can be like opening a hornet's nest with a shovel. Officers will rarely admit publicly that they made a mistake on a traffic collision report. Before you jump to any conclusions about their self-serving ego-protection, keep a few other related factors in mind:

1. *Most officers would rather fight armed gangs barehanded than admit one of their reports is factually incorrect.* Completed police reports can take on the appearance of stone monuments. Once the report leaves the officer's hands, is approved by his or her supervisor, and heads to the Records Division dungeon, it becomes very difficult to retrieve, correct, and resubmit. This, however, should be the officer's problem and not yours. If you discover a bona fide error in any police report, you have the right, as the client's advocate, to request that the report be redone.

2. *The error-correction process makes nuclear physics appear simple.* Because most police agencies want their officers to do it right the first time, they make report-error correcting a tedious and time-consuming process. Again, this is not your worry, but rather the officer's. Just be aware that the steps to fix errors can take days or even weeks in some cases. First, the officer must retrieve the original copy of the old report from the Records Division; then he or she must show the offending report to a ranking supervisor and point out the error or errors that need correction.

   This can be particularly galling if the supervisor thinks the officer is in any way incompetent in the first place, and even more so if (as happens in small police departments) that same supervisor signed the report without catching the error either.

3. *The officer must rewrite the original report.* Armed with approval from above, the officer must go back to the scene (in the case of traffic collision report mistakes) or go back to his or her field notebook to review and rewrite the entire report. With the errors corrected, the officer resubmits both reports for

review and approval, along with a separate narrative that explains how and why he or she came to see these errors (from your phone call) and why they were corrected.

4. *The whole package goes back to Records for resorting and refiling.* This means it could sit in an in-basket for two days or two weeks while it waits to go back into the "system." Be prepared to wait for results. Between phone calls chasing the officer down and delays surrounding the resubmittal process, it could take you one month or longer to get a copy of the amended report. Stick to your guns, though. If you're right, you're right, and you should expect the officer to make changes to reflect the truth. Just don't think this whole procedure will take place overnight.

This entire process can either go smoothly or bog down in seemingly endless delays. Much depends on the police agency and on your personal relationship with someone there. If you find that you're playing rounds and rounds of "telephone tag" or are getting little if any help or movement from the officer, don't be shy about going over his or her head.

Police agencies are like military organizations, with a recognizable chain of command. Unlike a private business where you may have to make several calls to find the right person to help you, in a law enforcement agency you can go right to the source of the problem and above it if necessary.

Typically, a police or sheriff's department is staffed from the bottom to the top: officers (or deputies), sergeants, lieutenants, captains, commanders, deputy chiefs (or assistant sheriffs), and the chief (or sheriff).

If you're having problems working with an officer on a report or some other client-related matter, ask to speak to his or her immediate supervisor, the sergeant. If you don't get satisfaction after a reasonable amount of waiting, go over the sergeant's head to the lieutenant, and so on. Someone somewhere will light a fire under someone else and your problem will get some attention.

Remember that far more than those in most professions, law

enforcement officers stick together through thick and thin. Helping you show that another officer was wrong is not something most officers will leap to do, but they *will* do their job if you explain why it must be done.

Handling Difficult Cases

With few exceptions, police officers are humane, caring folks who only want to do their jobs safely and effectively and go home in one piece at the end of the day. Notice that the phrase "their jobs" does not include the phrase "your job" anywhere in it. They probably will not work at breakneck speed to assist you. Your concerns and your responsibilities to your law firm are not their top priority. They will do their jobs and be as professional as they can, but some cases are significantly more trying and emotionally difficult than others.

Sometimes it's difficult for police officers to conceal or control their true feelings during difficult cases: murders of young women or children, murders of fellow cops, hideously violent rapes, child-related abuse or molestation cases, fatal accidents involving children, etc.

If you work for a criminal defense firm, a personal injury firm, or a civil litigation firm that handles high-profile arrests, traffic death cases, or police civil suits, be prepared to face a wide range of emotions when you deal with the officers involved. Here's a case that illustrates how these emotions can affect you as a paralegal.

In 1988, in San Diego, California, patrol officers responded to an "officer needs help" call to find an SDPD officer fatally shot in the head after he had run after some drug-dealing gang members. The suspects fled into the night, thereby initiating an intense manhunt to find the dead officer's killer. By the time the shooting suspect was captured the next day, over 250 officers had participated in the case.

Each officer wrote a short report that documented his or her activities—traffic control, scene protection, SWAT work, command post mobile van operations, etc.

When the case came to trial over three years later, the defense attorney assigned to handle the shooting suspect's case subpoenaed all of the officers on the scene as possible defense witnesses. As the trial date approached, officers were told by their department to call the defense attorney's paralegal staff and advise their status (vacation, days off, etc.) for the trial.

Imagine the hostility, overt and covert, these paralegals encountered as they spoke with each of these several hundred obviously upset police officers. Most of the officers were at least polite as they "checked in" with the defendant's attorney, but you know some of them could not contain their anger or resentment and took it out on the paralegals assigned to monitor their participation in the case.

As you handle difficult or highly charged cases involving death, injury, children, sex crimes, etc., try to keep your perspective and that of the officers involved in the back of your mind. Don't personalize any negative feelings they may have toward you just because you're trying to do a complete and professional job.

There are an estimated 523,000 police officers in this country. Make friends with a few of them if you can. Always strive to build a professional rapport with certain officers who can give you valuable assistance. If they know they can trust you as a fair person who will not try to humiliate them, trick them, or belittle their efforts, you'll reap a wide range of information and assistance.

Having a good reputation with your local police as an upfront member of the legal community will go a long way toward helping your career. You never know when a case will come across your desk that you can solve with a simple phone call to an officer who knows your work.

Working with Private Investigators (PIs)

One of the most popular television programs of the 1970s and early '80s was "The Rockford Files." This comedy-drama private detective show still exists in syndication and remains a high watermark for this TV genre. Besides the usual weekly follies and foibles involving veteran actor James Garner, the show usually focused on Jim's relationship with harried LAPD detective Dennis Becker, played by Joe Santos.

Dennis was forever taking Jim's phone calls, running his license plates, checking out his criminals in the police computer, and showing up to fish him out of jail when things went bad. The poor officer spent the rest of his time trying to appease his crabby boss and carefully planning his arrival to show up in the nick of time to save his buddy Jim from harm.

The idea of the cop befriending the private investigator is not new to television or the movies. These relationships range from true friendship to near hate and disgust for each other. The theme is usually constant: The private detective butts heads with the police as he searches for information. Using brains, skills, and the made-for-TV luck that few police officers have access to, our hero uncovers the true perpetrators of the crime several dangerous minutes before the police stumble onto the same conclusion and show up conveniently to save his bacon in time for another episode.

These shows try to show each character, cop and PI, with a grudging admiration or respect for the other. Shows like "Spenser: For Hire," "Magnum, P.I.," "The Equalizer," and old favorites like "Mannix," "Barnaby Jones," and "Cannon" have followed this plot line since Day One. But while we know life often imitates art, does this relationship of mutual need really exist in the PI world? The answer is a carefully qualified "yes."

You probably can guess that in most cities where private investigators choose to work, they have sprung from the ranks of some nearby law enforcement agency. This connection is logically linked to PI licensing requirements in most states. Just to qualify to take their state-controlled PI test, most applicants must prove they have had a full-time law enforcement, insurance investigation, or legal background. Some people qualify because they have served a sort of "apprenticeship" as employees of a licensed PI or insurance investigation firm, but most come to the job after they retire from or leave their law enforcement positions.

As such, their link to their old agency is no surprise. A twenty-five-year police officer who opens his own PI business probably can count on various overt or covert favors from his old pals who still wear badges. Retired agents from the FBI, IRS, DEA, and other Treasury Department agencies also may call in some "markers" from time to time. Is this legal? Not usually. Is it frowned upon? You bet. Does it still exist? Yes.

The way each side justifies this misuse of information and other confidential assets is by claiming that it's in the interest of "justice." In most instances, the fraud-trained PI who calls his pal in the Records Division for a little information about a man who wants to buy his client's business is probably only trying to protect the client's interests and earn his fee by providing valuable information. The accident-reconstruction PI who gets registered owner and license plate information from his friends on patrol is only trying to help his attorney client expedite a personal injury settlement. And the criminal defense PI who calls upon a detective friend to learn if other charges are pending against the client is only trying to protect the attorney from any surprises.

While this behavior goes on in degrees ranging from the rare to the outrageous, two things should concern you: Can the PIs who work for your firm get access to information that could truly help your case? More importantly, can they get this information in a legal, ethical, and timely manner?

The best way to find out about what they can get and what and who they know is to ask them. Since the private investigator business is a highly competitive, low-profit–margin business, most PIs who work as outside contractors or consultants for attorneys are only too happy to tell you what you want to hear. Some of the less scrupulous ones will say and do anything, legal or otherwise, to keep your account.

Like most private enterprise workers, PIs tend to think and act as it relates to their wallets. Since they earn most of their money based on billing hours and flat rate work—rather than by full-time employment with a law firm or under a retainer arrangement—they tend to be motivated largely by their desire to make the most money in the least amount of time.

While this is a perfectly normal way to approach the free enterprise business system we all know and love, it can interfere with good judgement if it gets out of hand. Unchecked by high moral standards and clear ethical values, too much money-chasing can create liability, reputation, or malpractice problems for the individual investigator, the firm for which he or she works, and the attorney who has contracted for investigative services.

If your firm needs the services of a good investigator, concentrate on establishing some hiring guidelines, selection criteria, and work-relationship standards before you hire anyone. The woods are full of PIs, and it only helps everyone concerned to make a careful selection, verify the work rules, and give guidance and support to the one you choose.

If your firm already employs an in-house or outside investigator, you may want to evaluate him or her based on certain key issues. Remember that malpractice as it relates to PIs under your firm's direction or locus of control can come back to haunt you later. Consider the following important issues when working with any PI firm:

1. *Is the firm licensed by your state? Insured with proper malpractice and other business insurance related to what its investigators do?* Private investigators' licenses work differently in each state, but no matter what the rules and regulations are for the individual PI, each PI firm you do business with should be licensed and insured.

   In some states, each person must have a license to be considered a "private investigator," while in others, employees may work under a "manager's" license while they earn enough hours to qualify for their own licenses.

   Make sure the firm you choose is licensed. Ask for its state license number and spend some time verifying it as accurate. A small amount of research can save your firm from embarrassing moments on the witness stand, as when opposing counsel asks your investigator, "By the way, are you licensed in this state?" and hears a sheepish "no" as a reply. This can damage your credibility, ruin your firm's reputation, and kill a perfectly good case for your client.

   Further, unlicensed PIs are usually uninsured as well, and this could bring financial ruin down on you should they commit malpractice while under your direction.

2. *What is the firm's reputation within the PI community? The legal community? With the local police?* Some PI firms have a sterling reputation amongst their peers, other attorneys, and even local law enforcement agencies. They work in a timely, professional, and ethical manner, leaving no stone unturned to get the job done, but always in a legal way. They have grudging respect from fellow PIs for their skills (and ability to get and keep new clients), high praise from their attorney clients for their case-saving work, and good grades from local law enforcement authorities for not interfering in ongoing felony cases (which is against the law in many states) or for offering to share information they've collected with the police.

But just as there are good PIs in the business world, there are also some cave-dwellers who help give the entire industry a black eye. These individuals are often unlicensed and are working out of their homes or the corner phone booth. Even if they are licensed, they may be highly unethical. They will do or say anything to an attorney to get hired, and they will often do or say anything to get information on a case.

These so-called shortcuts can mean problems later, especially when you discover that the PI you hired to take a witness statement typed up a half-baked version of what the witness saw, forged the witness's signature, and turned it in as a bona fide document to go into the client's case file.

When you go to bring this PI in for a deposition or a hearing, he has either skipped town, forgotten where he put the file, or worse, will lie under oath, all for his hourly fee.

Just as there are horror stories surrounding unscrupulous lawyers, you'll find an equal number of stories about shoddy, crooked, or just plain ignorant PIs who try to pass themselves off as professionals. Good PIs know there is no easy road to the truth; conscientious PIs may be willing to put in nights and weekends to find out all they can for you.

Word of mouth is usually the best way to find a trustworthy private investigator. Ask other attorneys and other paralegals who they use and schedule an appointment to hear a presentation from them. Professional PI firms will be happy to put on a well-polished presentation for your attorneys explaining their methods, reports, and fees.

3. *How long has the firm been in business?* Studies of small businesses show that it usually takes from three to five years for any small business to get its feet firmly planted on the ground. After this point, most of the learning process is over, the employee and workload problems have been ironed out, and the business is strong enough to survive.

PI firms offer no exception to this rule. While newer firms may offer low rates and seem eager for your business, they may have some behind-the-scenes problems you don't know about. Smaller, newer PI firms tend to live "on the edge," cashing attorneys' checks at the bank as fast as they get them. They also may have an air of desperation about them because money may be tight. While they may provide good service in their eagerness to keep you as a client, money concerns may cloud their judgement.

For best results, choose a well-established firm that specializes in your types of cases. It has probably earned its experience with other smaller law firms and has moved up to a more powerful clientele.

4. *What is the background and experience of the PIs on staff? Law enforcement, insurance, engineering?* Some PIs specialize in specific subjects. Their law enforcement backgrounds may have taught them criminal investigation techniques, auto crash analysis methods, or financial searching skills.

Other PIs may have worked as adjusters for large insurance companies and then have gone out on their own to start their businesses. They may have tremendous experience with car crash cases; worker's compensation settlements; medical, legal, or professional malpractice cases; or a variety of other insurance-based claims. Their expertise could be highly valuable as an aid to settlement.

Lastly, ask if the PIs have qualified in court as expert witnesses and under what subjects they qualify, e.g., traffic accident investigation, narcotics, drunk driving enforcement, police use of force, fraud cases, etc. Make sure you can verify this information before you go to court. Imagine how much time and effort you would waste if the other side were to disqualify your investigator as an expert in court. Always find out these things first.

5. *What specific training do staff investigators have?* Be ready to read their resumes—also called their "curriculum vitae"—to get an idea of their education, training, work experience, and work history. Some PIs will stress law enforcement credentials, while others will highlight their graduate engineering degrees. Others may have worked in similar investigative-type positions for the federal government, e.g., airplane crash experts, rail car crash investigators, Food and Drug Administration inspectors, etc.

   Some firms may offer themselves as full-service investigators, with a staff of several people with differing skills and talents.

6. *What kinds of services can the PI firm offer your firm?* Here's a short list of some things a full-service PI firm will provide for you: background checks, asset searches, criminal investigations, civil investigations, accident reconstruction, family law case investigations, skip traces and locates, surveillance with photos or video, financial crime investigations, worker's compensation investigations, and polygraph work.

   The best way to get high-quality reports is to choose certified experts in their field. Ask what each PI is qualified to do and choose from there.

7. *What is the fee structure? Billing minimums? Payment terms?* Don't settle for second-rate investigators. Good help is not cheap, but even higher-than-average costs can be cost-effective if the efforts lead to a better success rate for you.

   Most investigators charge by the hour, usually $25 to $100, plus expenses. Some PIs work on a monthly retainer system, with whatever money is not used credited to the next month. Most work on a case-by-case basis, setting fixed prices for records checks, interviews, photos, etc.

It's a good idea to create a letter of agreement about payment terms in advance of any work. Spell out exactly what you expect in terms of material from the PI and when and how you will pay the bills. A PI will typically collect from attorney clients on a bi-weekly or month's-end basis, turning in each report as he or she completes it, with a complete invoice explaining the time, fees, and expenses.

8. *Does the firm offer references? Testimonials? Samples of past work?* Talk to other attorneys and paralegals about their PIs and look for a glowing recommendation. Get some sample reports, photos, diagrams, models, etc. from the PI to review with your attorneys. Ask representatives from the firm to talk about the last time they testified in court and the results of their testimony. Get a feel for what they do, how competent they've been in the past, and how much they charge before you give them any work. Good PI firms will stand up to close scrutiny. Shady firms won't and shouldn't get your business anyway.

Helping the Private Investigator

In many law offices, the paralegal acts as the point of contact for the private investigator. The PI gets his or her case assignments from the paralegal, including: copies of the client's police report, medical records, names and telephone numbers for witnesses, and a complete set of marching orders for the case—what to tackle first, when to complete the work, and any limits on fees, deadlines, or other significant issues.

Many PIs work on an on-call basis, coming into the law office only to pick up new cases or drop off completed reports. While there, they may have an opportunity to chat with the paralegal about various new cases, but in many busy offices, they must rely on the paralegal's written notes and instructions before they proceed.

Here's a message from a private investigator, Joe Coyle from Joe

Coyle and Associates, a San Diego–based firm that handles civil investigations, accident reconstruction, expert witness testimony, and skip tracing.

"This written communication process," says investigator Joe Coyle, "must be as complete as possible. The more I know about the case going in, the easier it is for me to get it done. Since I charge by the hour, the faster I can work, the less expensive it is for the firm."

He further adds, "The paralegal should try to give me everything he or she knows about the case, including notes from the client's interview, any witness information, and what issues the attorney handling the case seeks to prove or disprove. If I know about certain important areas the attorney wants covered, I can focus my attention on them."

Coyle says not to worry about giving him too much paperwork. "I can sort through what helps me and what doesn't. In some cases, even the smallest piece of information has helped me tremendously."

"Most good PIs," adds Coyle, "will check in with the paralegal or the attorney on a regular basis. This keeps everyone aware of any changes or surprises in the case and can point out new directions if necessary. I always call my attorney clients if I run into a case problem that may require a great deal of my time and effort to handle. This gives them the option of telling me to continue or wrap it up at that point."

Helping the Process Server

Some private investigators are also licensed process servers, and this combination of talents can help you take a case from the beginning stages all the way to the courtroom.

Review the section above concerning the selection criteria for your private investigators and use the same themes to choose a process server. Although the server's work may be less detailed or expensive than that of the investigator, it's often just as critical to the success of the case. Unserved or wrongly served defendants can cause huge scheduling delays and damage an otherwise well-planned case.

As with investigators, use word-of-mouth referrals and recommendations from other attorneys and paralegals to choose an effective server. Some attorney service firms do a high-volume business, serving and filing several hundred papers per day. While these cost-effective firms may be useful for "ordinary" services, they may not handle harder jobs. Other firms may specialize in difficult services and locates, and the price of their work is reflected in the degree of difficulty.

If you could ask for three words to help choose a good process server, they would be: reliability, reliability, and reliability. Process servers literally hold the future of your case in their hands. Their ability to find and serve the defendant should be matched by their speed and accuracy in filing the proof-of-service forms. You don't need lazy, sloppy, or money-hungry process servers ruining potentially good cases for your firm with their shortcuts, unethical behavior, or rules violations.

There are plenty of good stories about crafty servers who use perfectly legal methods to catch their defendants unawares. One celebrated process server learned his defendant liked to take morning swims in the ocean. He waited until she was rinsing off in an outdoor shower near the beach parking lot before he served her with civil papers wrapped in a well-sealed plastic bag.

Another veteran process server waited all day in an office lobby for a child-support defendant to appear. This person knew a process server was after him and had taken to sprinting away if anyone even called him by name. On this day, however, the process server had a picture of the defendant and called to him as he crossed the office lobby. The defendant ran for an open, empty elevator car, but the server got there at the same time. He tossed the papers at the defendant's feet and said, "You've been served!" as the elevator doors closed around him.

Above all else, choose an aggressive server with good people skills, plenty of patience, and a head for details and accuracy. And as with your private investigators, never ask a process server to lie about serving someone, cheat the court filing rules, break any laws, or otherwise jeopardize a case just to serve someone.

Here's a message from one licensed process server, Rhys Danylyshyn-Adams, owner of Attorney Service West, a San Diego–based process service and private investigation firm. Besides specializing in hard-to-locate and hard-to-serve defendants, he also conducts background checks, asset searches, and skip traces.

Danylyshyn-Adams is a veteran process server who goes out of his way to make paralegals' lives easier. He gives all his clients a four-copy carbonless form to fill out for each process service. He asks his paralegal clients to type the form completely, adding additional or special instructions as necessary. Here's a brief primer on what most process servers expect from paralegals:

"Fill out the form completely," he says. "The more I know about the defendant, the faster I can serve him or her. Make sure to give me the case number, the presiding court, and the full names of both the client and the defendant, as well as everything you know about the defendant, like the home and work addresses, home and work phone numbers, mailing addresses, and even a physical description, Social Security number, or driver's license number if it's going to be a difficult service."

He continues, "Please list all documents exactly as they should appear on the proof of service. List the defendant's name exactly as it is to appear on the proof of service. In some courts, if there are mistakes, the clerk will send the proof back with red pen marks all over it. You'll have to retype the whole thing and have it signed again if a letter, space, or comma is omitted."

Danylyshyn-Adams talks about special services: "It's fine to list a husband and wife on one form if they live at the same address. But if you have separate addresses for home and work, you need to list the wife to be served at the residence if she in fact does not work at the husband's business. All other people need to be listed on separate forms in case they are not at the home address and have left the business address.

"Make sure that all your instructions to the process server are clear and concise. Don't assume anything, as some servers will do only what is written for them and nothing more. Spell it out, like the total number of documents to be served in case one is misplaced."

As time is always a factor in process service, Danylyshyn-Adams suggests you mark all deadline dates as clearly as possible, circling them in red ink right on the forms. You should also type any instructions: "Call attorney when served," "Wait to file proof of service," or "Last day to serve or file," "Made two attempts already," etc. This tells the server exactly how and when to proceed and eliminates miscommunication problems later.

Sub-service cases also require special instructions. "If you want the papers to be sub-served, it's important to give an extra copy to the process server. Then he or she can mail the extra copy back to you."

Danylyshyn-Adams offers some suggestions for choosing a process service firm: "You need to know in your mind that the person who carries these important documents for your law firm is honest, sincere, prompt, and well-groomed. Each factor plays an important role in service of process.

"In this business, honesty is everything. It all comes down to a simple question: Did the process server really go to the defendant's home or work or did he or she just toss the papers in the trash? I've heard horror stories where certain process servers simply tossed out the papers and typed proofs of service, never intending to go to the addresses or make attempts.

"As a paralegal, you should keep close tabs as to what is going on with each service. Keep in contact with your process server and be organized. Keep a copy of the invoice from the process service company in the client's file as a permanent record."

Danylyshyn-Adams concludes by saying, "Most process servers want to do a good job for their clients. The more help and guidance you can give them at the start, the better the service will turn out, which is what really matters."

Working More Effectively with Insurance Adjusters

If you look at the broad legal picture, nearly everything regulated by civil law is also covered by some form of insurance. Whether it's a maritime shipping loss, a worker's compensation case, a car accident, a slip and fall in a shopping center, a homeowner's suit against a builder, a wrongful death case, a product liability case, or a medical or professional malpractice case, nearly everything involves a responsible insurance company as the party that finally pays any settlement bills.

In each of these events where an attorney represents an injured or aggrieved party, it's the insurance company—through its insurance defense lawyers or through an adjuster who works for it—that does the negotiating. Who negotiates on the client's behalf depends on the complexity and dollar amounts involved in the case. As the paralegal profession grows in stature and skill, more attorneys are turning over their high-volume, low-dollar-amount cases to their paralegals to negotiate and settle. This allows the attorneys more time to concentrate on the high-dollar, more specialized cases that need their full attention.

Here's a message from an independent insurance adjuster, William Bernstein, an adjuster and investigator from the southern California firm Schifrin, Gagnon & Dickey. Bernstein is a veteran adjuster, with over 30 years in the business. Over his long career, he has worked as an investigator and adjuster for individual attorneys, large law firms, insurance companies, and even self-insured companies. He has settled cases ranging from fatal car accidents to slip and falls in restaurants and from wrongful deaths to product liability.

"Knowing how adjusters think and what is important to them is the key to any negotiating session. As much as the adjuster wants to believe your client, remember that he or she is looking to save the insurance company money. Adjusters' decisions are almost always based upon how much things will cost them."

Bernstein suggests you try to take a friendly, professional approach in any negotiation. The active listening skills discussed in Chapter 2 apply to your conversations with adjusters. Listen to their side, take notes during the conversation, and wait until they've finished before you present your case.

"Trying to come on too strong or trying to 'steamroll' the adjuster will just defeat your purpose," Bernstein says. "He or she knows you're trying to get the most you can for your client. Stick to the issues, like the dollar figures for the injuries, property damage, lost work time, etc. Keep personality issues out of it and try not to antagonize the adjuster with lawsuit threats, loud arguments, or accusations of bad faith."

Bernstein says most paralegals run into trouble when they get in over their heads. "Keep your dollar figure limits in mind as you discuss a case with the adjuster. If your numbers are vastly different from the adjuster's, and the negotiation is getting out of hand, step back and tell the other side you need to talk with the attorney and the client before you can proceed.

"Keep your eye on the ball," he adds. "Never forget that you represent the client first, and your objective is to get the most money for his or her claim. Some paralegals let their emotions get away from them so that personality conflicts with the adjuster spoil the negotiation. Remember, it's not your case, it's the client's case. Make a fair and reasonable offer and be willing to negotiate with the adjuster about it. Arguments only waste everyone's time and prevent the case from settling in a reasonable fashion."

He adds that few things irritate an adjuster more than receipt of a client's medical bills that obviously have been "padded" by the attorney and the doctor working on the case. "Don't expect much sympathy from an adjuster if the client has a minor accident that caused $200 worth of property damage and then submits medical bills worth $5,000 from the treating doctor. The adjuster will agree to settle the case only if his or her side was at fault and if the dollar figures make reasonable sense."

In those rare cases where personalities do collide or the adjuster is being completely unreasonable during the negotiating process, Bernstein suggests you go over the adjuster's head to his or her supervisor. "Sometimes the supervisor can intervene in the case and break the deadlocks between you. Other times, the supervisor will agree to some concessions just to get the case settled. Because he or she may have more leeway than the adjuster, you may be able to come to a more reasonable agreement than you thought was possible.

"In all cases," says Bernstein, "be fair and professional. Be polite, stay flexible, and keep your client's best interests in mind at all times. If you find yourself stuck on certain key issues, you may want to bring in the attorney to close the negotiation. Sometimes a new voice will help put things in a new light. Adjusters usually want to settle a bona fide case at some reasonable amount because they know going to court is an expensive and time-consuming process. But in those cases where you know the courtroom is the only place to settle the matter, stick to your guns if you know your side is right."

Negotiating your own cases can represent the pinnacle of your achievement as a paralegal. Only top-flight professionals are afforded this opportunity and this comes only after they've proven their competence and worth to their attorneys.

Using Expert Witnesses

The old saying "You have to spend money to make money" applies when using expert witnesses. High-powered experts are rarely cheap, but their expertise, subject knowledge, and courtroom testimony skills can turn your case from an apparent loser into a big-money winner.

This financial paradox exists because good expert witnesses know that with their brain power they can command high fees for their court time. This should tell you something your attorneys probably learned early in law school: Get your expert witnesses on the stand quickly and get them off early. Experts may charge between $100 and $1000 per hour, and the meter is running even when they're cooling their heels in the hallways of the courthouse. Long trials and lengthy delays can create sky-high expert witness bills.

But cost concerns aside, using qualified experts can mean all the difference in a civil or criminal trial. Since the experts make their livings thinking on their feet, they can sway a jury to your side with only a few power-packed minutes of testimony.

Finding experts can be a hit-or-miss proposition. While you can find specific experts through their ads in various attorneys' magazines, word-of-mouth referrals tend to offer better results. Check the experts' credentials, ask for samples of their trial work, and research their past cases for proof of their courtroom competence.

When an expert witness accepts a case, he or she will need two things to succeed: time and information. You may have the luxury of one but not the other, but if possible, you should give the experts the advantage of a complete case file to review, enough time for them to prepare a court-acceptable report of their findings, and enough time to get themselves ready to testify.

In high-profile criminal cases, the psychologists, evidence experts, medical experts, police experts, and other similar professionals can turn the entire case around on the basis of a single day's testimony. Try to give them the benefit of time as an ally rather than an enemy.

Expert witnesses are like snowflakes: Each one is different and each one is unique. I recall one expert witness whose entire career is based upon his knowledge of trees and how and why they fall to the ground, injuring people or damaging property.

Other experts specialize in mining accidents, jet aircraft crashes, train freight-car derailments, metallurgical failures, construction crane accidents, multiple-personality disorders, birth defects, police defensive tactics training, high-speed automobile driving, accidental firearms discharges, electrical fires, and even biological household contaminations. The list of available experts is nearly endless and is limited only to your type of case and the results your attorneys are looking for.

Good outside help—whether it comes from private investigators, process servers, independent adjusters, or expert witnesses—can add significant value to many of your cases. Their support, expertise, and ability to take the "helicopter view" (seeing each case from above as a disinterested third party) is usually worth far more than their fees.

five

WORKING THE CASE:
How to Do Your Own Thorough Research and Investigation

"Research is to see what everybody else has seen, and to think what nobody else has thought."—Albert Szent-Gyorgyi

*A*ttorneys' reputations are made and lost by how they handle their cases. The same can also be said for paralegals. How you take a case from the initial client meeting to the settled and closed status shows every person in your office your abilities, skills, knowledge, determination, and commitment to be the client's service advocate.

And while some cases almost handle themselves because they are relatively straightforward, others require a tremendous effort on the part of everyone in your firm to complete. Some cases flow along at a fast clip, with meetings, conferences, settlement discussions, and court appearances coming and going on the office calendar as if attached to the jetstream. In these fortunate matters, the clients, defendants, attorneys, associated legal professionals, outside agencies, and the justice system all stay out of each other's way and get the case finished in a satisfactory amount of time for all concerned.

But other cases seem more like "tar babies," sticking to you and the other attorneys involved and refusing to let go. Countless hours of work and effort move them along to resolution by only a few fractions of an inch, while the size of the file itself grows by feet and yards. But just as the attorneys earn their fees on these "groaners," so do you earn your salary.

Difficult, time-consuming, or highly emotional cases are the exception rather than the rule in most law firms. However, their mere presence can cause unproductive and unhealthy shifts in the work load distribution, time management policies, and energy levels in the entire firm. Facing large, hard cases can be daunting, especially if you feel uncertain about the elements involved.

So what's the solution? Throw in the towel? Pass the tough cases off to other paralegals, other attorneys, or even other law firms? Not if you want to survive and thrive as a paralegal professional. The secret to handling potentially challenging cases is to follow the Boy Scouts' motto: Be Prepared!

The more work you can do in advance—at the beginning of the case, and as it progresses—the better off you'll be come "crunch time." While this sounds easy to say and hard to do, keep in mind that time is usually on your side at the start of the case. The more information you can gather, the more steps you can check off, the more physical "book and leg" work you can do at the start, the smoother the case will go, especially when deadlines, pressures, and other indicators of stress loom down the road.

Your role, as a paralegal professional, is to make your attorney's job easier. And since his or her job is to handle and settle cases and legal matters for clients, your "aide-de-camp" duties should entail most of the pick-and-shovel work for the case—preparing memos, calendaring dates, writing reminder notes, briefs, and client correspondence, etc.—without being asked, reminded, or cajoled by anyone else. The more you do for yourself early in the case, and the more you do for the attorney, the easier the case will become.

Paralegal Success Traits

Since most of your value as a paralegal professional stems from your case-handling, case-management abilities, you should already know that to get anywhere with even the most routine cases you must be able to dig, and dig, and dig some more for information. Go past the routine movements and push on; look for more information you can discover, verify, and add to the file.

You should already have set your sights on becoming a "case cracker"—someone who can find that one piece of information that puts the case over the winning edge. Any paralegal can handle the simplest and most routine chores; it's the pros who know what it takes to work past any arising difficulties to get the job done.

To become a case cracker, the sort of paralegal professional who tackles extraordinary cases with relish, you may need to make some visible changes in your work habits and even alter some of your personality traits. Here are some of the more important characteristics of case crackers:

- *Aggressiveness*—They have a "never quit" attitude and an unwillingness to give up on a lead, avenue of information, or problem until they have exhausted every effort. This is coupled with a desire to come to the office each day with specific goals in mind and ideas about ways to achieve those goals in a timely manner. Their phone skills are fully developed in such a way as to get the most information in the shortest amount of time. They stay focused on their tasks and don't get sidetracked by other distractions or discouraged by any obstacles that get in their way.

- *Ingenuity*—They have the ability to look for the seemingly "wild" solution or some unique alternative that gets the job done for them in a way most people thought wasn't possible. They aren't afraid to be inventive, slightly illogical, or even a shade outrageous to solve a complex problem with a completely new approach.

- *Creativity*—They tend to be highly innovative thinkers, able to see in more than one direction. Given a blank sheet of paper and a problem, they can come up with a large number of highly probable and effective solutions. They see things more in terms of many different channels rather than black-and-white, right-or-wrong approaches.

• *Big-picture thinking*—They have a marked ability to take the "helicopter view" of any problem. By seeing the forest AND the trees, they don't get caught up in any one part of the problem to the exclusion of all others. They can see the entire problem and propose worthwhile multipurpose solutions accordingly.

• *Tolerance for ambiguity*—In a world filled with people who want the right answer, and yesterday at that, they can wait patiently for information that fills in the entire picture. They can deal comfortably with unresolved, uncertain, or unfamiliar situations. These flexible people afford themselves an opportunity to delay their actions until they've studied the problem; they aren't committed to one solution at the expense of all others.

Traits like these separate merely good paralegals from great ones. Look at your own work habits and see if you can make some improvements in the way you tackle problems and anticipate approaching challenges.

Thinking and Acting Like an Investigator

A good PI tries to be a jack-of-all-trades, working not only as an investigator but also as a researcher, interviewer, analyzer, and lastly, a thinker. After getting a case from a law firm, a skilled investigator immediately prioritizes his or her tasks, thinking about where to start, who to contact for help, what issues to uncover, what potential problems to clear up, and how much time to spend doing research, talking by phone or in person to people, and chasing down other leads. This organizing process helps investigators save time and effort—not just theirs, but yours as well.

But while good investigators try to think of all the things they can do to complete a case, they also realize that to maximize their efforts they may need to "synergize" their approach. Some case-oriented tasks may be beyond their scope of expertise or knowledge, so they reach out into their large network of friends, colleagues, and peers to get good, qualified help with these various aspects. By coordinating the efforts of others, they can focus their activities on the parts of the case they feel best qualified to handle.

As an example, many investigators who work for personal injury and traffic-collision firms have some limited background in traffic-accident scene examination. This basic knowledge may carry them through dozens of traffic cases with few problems. But in more complex or serious cases, perhaps involving deaths, multiple cars, and multiple serious injuries or extensive amounts of complicated physical evidence like skid marks, scrapes, or equipment failures, these same competent investigators may need to call on colleagues with even more training.

Typically, accident reconstructionists have proven backgrounds in engineering, physics, vehicle accident characteristics, tire wear and skid mark evaluation, and even metallurgy. These highly trained reconstructionists become the investigator's own "expert witnesses," helping discover the truth in difficult cases where the weight of evidence is too overwhelming and important to leave to chance.

Just as some attorneys go outside their firms to hire veteran trial lawyers to take their cases to court, a good investigator will know his or her boundaries of knowledge and call on others for assistance when necessary.

As another example, if the investigator is asked to conduct a complete asset search of a defendant, he or she may call upon a colleague with access to bank accounts, stock portfolios, real estate, or similar financial instruments. This associate, who deals in these areas on a regular basis, can get far more accomplished, and in less time, than the investigator.

And so it should go with you as the paralegal professional. From the beginning of your career, gather names of people who can help you later. A paralegal who spends a few hours per month networking with colleagues in various legal, social, and professional organizations and attending society and association meetings can come away with a vast library of resources, all contained on single two-inch by three-and-one-half-inch pieces of paper known as business cards.

Be prepared to collect business cards and to give yours out in any social situation that may relate to your profession. Your goal should be to collect at least one Rolodex™ file, if not two, of competent professionals who may be able to give you assistance at some time in the future.

It's been said that you are only three or four phone calls away from anyone you would ever want to meet. A case in point: I have an associate who is on friendly terms with the personal accountant for a United States Senator. I have another friend who is a U.S. Secret Service agent, assigned to the Washington, DC, presidential protection squad. Should I ever seriously wish to meet our President (assuming I could get to the White House and his schedule-makers could find a spare five minutes), I only have to make a few calls to start the wheels in motion.

While this example may sound a bit fantastic, it would be possible to achieve that outcome if I really wanted to undertake it.

The point is that many of your obstacles to help and information are self-imposed. By expanding your network of qualified associates, you can develop a personal list of people who may be of help to you tomorrow, next year, or in five years. The beauty of this well-stocked list is that the people whose names are in it represent a huge source of untapped energy at your disposal. It's not necessary to call everyone in your phone list once a week to check in, but rather, once a year, go through it and call the people you haven't encountered on a regular basis. Find out if they are still doing the same things. They may have changed jobs, changed careers, or perhaps have moved into your own office building.

As I look through my own full phone list, I see names and numbers for specialists of every type. If I were working as a paralegal today, I could call on: a friend who specializes in copyright law, an expert in electrical construction matters, a real estate appraiser, an engineer, a newspaper reporter, a banker, a polygraph operator, a chiropractor, a stamp collection expert, a forensic photographer, a video camera operator, a jewelry appraiser, a firefighter, a labor relations expert, a bus accident expert, a psychologist, a police homicide detective, a helicopter pilot, a computer security analyst, a hypnotist, a mortician, a postal worker, a tax expert, a chemist, and a sports injury therapist.

Do you think even one of these 25 experts could help me if I were a paralegal working on a personal injury, criminal defense, product liability, worker's compensation, civil, or business law case? If you were a paralegal who might be faced with any cases like these, wouldn't it be worthwhile to save the business cards of all these contacts for just the right set of circumstances? Yes!

This is not to say that everyone you meet will be able to further your career, lighten your caseload, or make you look like a star in front of your boss. But who's to say that someday, some time, you won't come across the one person who has a unique job or specialized training that can save you hours, days, or even weeks worth of time on a case. You can start this whole process by digging through your phone list and making a call. Keep the power of this network-oriented approach in the back of your mind at all times. Give out as many business cards as you collect and start to develop business relationships now so that they may pay dividends down the road.

Reading More, Listening More, Talking Less

What constitutes the "real" truth is often hard to pin down in legal matters. The client, the defendant, and the attorneys for each side are hardly disinterested or dispassionate third-party observers. Their status as case participants always gives them an important stake in the proceedings. As such, their opinions and beliefs can get skewed by their positions in the case. In worst-case scenarios, the truth gets confused by what important people—judges, attorneys, juries, adjusters, etc.—may *want* to hear. The facts are often obscured by unconscious interpretations.

Sometimes the only people who can rescue a sinking case from a series of accusations, arguments, and outright lies are the independent witnesses. Your role as a paralegal calls for you to be able to read "between the lines" of a written witness statement and dig deeply into what was said about the events in question.

Taking client, defendant, and witness statements at face value offers you only one side of the story. You must know how to get to the root of the matter through intelligent questioning skills.

If you're having problems settling a case, go back over the file for more help. Look at the statements and depositions made by all the parties. Spot the verbal clues, apparent misstatements, bald lies, and other issues that can give you a toehold into a new part of the case.

Don't be afraid to start again from the beginning. Make phone calls to your witnesses and re-interview them if you have questions after the first pass. Many new issues can have arisen in the weeks or months since you took a statement. Maybe you neglected an important detail; maybe some new information has changed the focus of the case; or maybe your investigator didn't cover a key area to your satisfaction.

When you ask your questions again, find out if the witness knows of any other people who might have seen what he or she saw. While this may seem like an obvious question, you'd be surprised at how many times you'll hear the witness say, "Oh, yeah, the barber who was cutting my hair at the time of the car accident looked out the window when I did. He didn't talk to the cops because he was busy with other customers."

Don't just rely on reports or other outside sources for your information; look for the answers yourself. For a traffic collision case, drive by the scene of the accident; take a look at the defendant's car if it's parked legally on the street; talk to the officer who took the police report; get a feel for the road and weather conditions at the time of the crash; see things from the client's car position, from the defendant's car position, and from the spot where the witness saw the accident.

In a crime case, go to the scene and reenact the events in your mind; look at the positions of people, fixed objects, barriers, and other distractions that may have kept the police, witnesses, or other accusers from seeing what they said they saw. Get a feel from inside yourself as to what happened and how it happened.

In less dramatic cases, those that take place on paper, read the complaints of both parties, study their documentation of the proof, and put yourself in the other's position. Maybe you can see a chance of a new defense, a new argument, or a new way of answering a previously unanswered problem.

Rely on your outside, impartial observers for more help. Most people want to help you and will give you more than enough information if you only ask for it in a polite and professional manner. You may learn of other interested bystanders, third parties who might contribute to your understanding of the case, and even the proverbial "little old lady who was outside watering her petunias when she saw the whole thing happen."

Learn to be more like a bulldog, seizing an important issue based on discussions with your attorney and really striving to pin it down before the case goes to court and before the other side learns about it first. Be polite, but don't take "no" for an answer when you're dealing with reluctant witnesses. If you can persuade them that their help is important, you can often turn an entire case around.

Remember to keep the big picture in mind and focus on your short- and long-term goals, as well as on those of your attorney.

Different Strokes for Different Folks

If everyone were as friendly, flexible, and cooperative as you are, it would be much easier to get your job done. Many people will help you if your requests aren't too time-consuming for them, but still it's better to be aware how they think and how they operate before you ask for their assistance.

Did you ever hear someone say about someone else, "He and I just don't seem to be communicating," or "She and I don't seem to be on the same wavelength"? These revealing statements point out that the way we communicate with each other is based on our perceptions of ourselves and of them.

Different people have different personality types. There are: pragmatic "drivers" who want to get things done in a hurry; amiable "sociables" who like people and enjoy talking about a variety of subjects over and above what you want; and methodical, "analytical" people who prefer to think about things, and use facts, figures, and models to help guide their choices. How effectively you deal with each one of these types, either as a client in your office or as a witness over the phone, depends heavily on your ability to communicate in different ways.

Instead of trying to force everyone to think and react as you do—not unlike forcing a square peg into a round hole—you should learn to adapt to their personality types. You don't have to be clairvoyant to divine most personality styles because most people reveal themselves by what they say and what they do. You can discover the answers to how they think and feel in their personal habits and verbal clues.

"Drivers" tend to be action-oriented people. A typical "driver" witness will want to know who you are, what you're calling about, and what you want to know, all in the space of about forty seconds. These people tend to be more aggressive than most and may be a bit more impulsive in their decision-making processes.

Since they have a "let's do it now" attitude, the worst way to appeal to drivers is through long-winded explanations of what you want or need from them. Ask them your questions and then step back and wait for their answers.

If you have "drivers" for clients, the best way to help them help you is briefly to explain the procedures surrounding their cases and wait for their questions. They'll tell you what is important to them with a minimum of wasted time. Drivers tend to be less concerned with social niceties like the weather, the local news, or any other topics that they see as diverting their time or energy away from real issues.

To interview "driver" clients and witnesses, act as they do. Be specific; ask clear questions they can answer easily; and don't try to waste their time.

"Sociables" are on the other side of the personality scale from "drivers." "Sociables" tend to like people and have no trouble carrying on a long conversation about unrelated topics before they get to the business at hand. They tend to be more chatty and friendly than "drivers," with a more positive outlook that may be revealed in their bright style of dress, enthusiastic tone of voice, or their genuine concern for you and your problems.

Whereas "drivers" need little prodding to tell their story and move on, "sociables" may need some careful guidance to stay on the subject and not drift off to other side issues that only complicate or delay things. "Sociables" also tend to think everyone else is like them and can get offended easily if you don't take the time to build rapport or establish a positive relationship before you begin questioning them.

You can recognize "sociables" by their need to have you set the stage for them before they start answering questions. They have to feel good about you before they open up and tell you what they know. If you have "sociables" for clients and as witnesses, the worst thing you can do is try to speed them along or give their attempts at relationship-building an apparent brush-off.

Lastly, "analyticals" tend to be much more pragmatic and closed than either "drivers" or "sociables." They have a tendency to hold their cards close to the chest until they can analyze the related parts. "Analyticals" need to know the facts before they proceed. They like to read things and look at data in their hands before offering an opinion.

If you have an "analytical" as a witness to a traffic collision, let him or her look at the police report before you ask any questions. "Analytical" business clients will have plenty of hard copy for you to put into the file. They will give you charts, reports, graphs, maps, and other visual, fact-based models from their files. They expect to get as much "paper" from you as they give, for this helps them put their conceptual hunches in order.

The worst way to deal with "analyticals" is to ask for an immediate answer without giving them enough time to read the facts, sort them out, and prepare a conclusion for you. Whereas "drivers" tend to want to make snap decisions based on their gut feelings, and "sociables" tend to want to establish a positive relationship before they begin, "analyticals" want time to look at the issues on paper, use their pens to make some notes or a sketch, and then give you their feedback.

Notice the key word "tend" that runs throughout each description of "drivers," "sociables," and "analyticals." These are only generalizations that we make about a person's personality type. In truth, most people are a combination of all three types. But while we each carry strengths and weaknesses from all three types, most people tend to gravitate to one distinct (and recognizable) style.

Even if you know very little initially about the concept of personality types and different thinking styles, you probably can make accurate guesses about the three we've discussed: "drivers" tend to communicate quite well with other "drivers"; "sociables" can communicate best with other "sociables"; and "analyticals" understand other "analyticals" best of all.

Knowing how to recognize these personality styles and being able to respond to them in a way that puts the other person at ease is your key to successful human interaction. Spotting noticeable trends in someone's personality can help you deal with clients, witnesses, and even your colleagues and co-workers on a more balanced and productive basis.

Doing Legal Research

The ability to do effective legal research is like any other learned skill; it takes effort and hands-on practice to get good at it. Whether you do your research in the local law library, at an on-campus law school library, or inside your own firm, you need to have a plan before you begin. Without a clear idea of where to start, what to look for, where to look for it, and how to document what you've found, you may end up spinning your wheels and wasting valuable time.

Doing legal research can be daunting. Civil and criminal cases grow exponentially by the day, and law libraries are crammed to the ceiling with supplements explaining new rulings and new issues. While some paralegals relish the challenge of a good "case hunt," others equate legal research with doing time in a torture chamber.

Your own positive or negative feelings about research may stem from the nature of the formal training you received on the subject. If you were fortunate enough to learn from a skilled professional—in school, in a paralegal training program, or from a qualified colleague—consider yourself lucky. With the mounting number of cases filling our law libraries, the best time to learn legal research is now while you can still squeeze in through the file-stacked doorway.

If your skills are a bit lacking, or if you feel overwhelmed by the process, take steps to overcome your "researchophobia" before it interferes with your career development. The shortcomings that will hurt your advancement most are communication problems, either oral or written, and an inability to find information in a timely manner for a harried boss.

To give your research skills a dusting-off, start with some of the available books on the subject. Read up on the best way to browse effectively in a law library and then start practicing. Go on your own time to your local law library and ask for help from the people who work there. Your request for assistance is not new to them, so take advantage of their experience and ask for some guidance. Many of the people who work in our law libraries are also paralegals, law students, and attorneys themselves. By striking up a friendship with a law library employee, you can gain entrance into a vast "hidden" world. Your friend in the law library can get you access to research help, "shepardizing" help, copy machines, computer database time, phone help, and similar benefits available to other paralegal colleagues.

Better still, if you have established a mentor relationship with a fellow paralegal or an attorney, ask your mentors for research help. If you show a willingness to learn and an appreciation of assistance, your mentors probably will be glad to show you the research tricks and shortcuts they've acquired over their legal careers.

If you work in a relatively small law office, you may not have much of a selection of law books to choose from. But even small offices will keep copies of the most important books for the practice—the state and federal codes.

These valuable tomes might be known under different names in your particular state, but they include:

• The state Penal Code—Explains the elements, violations, sentences, and statutes regulating crime and punishment.

- The state Vehicle Code—Explains the administrative, enabling, enforcement, and punishment statutes pertaining to motor vehicles.

- The city Municipal Code—Covers various laws and infractions specific to the community.

- The state Civil Code—Covers civil procedures.

- The state Business and Professions Code—Gives rules and regulations governing fair business practices and procedures.

- The state Welfare and Institutions—Covers state welfare issues, mental health concerns, juvenile protection, etc.

- The state Health and Safety Code—Covers occupational safety rules, narcotics violations, and state safety issues.

- The state Probate Code—Used to help determine will and probate cases.

- The state Real Estate Code—Governs real estate transactions with rules, regulations, and guidelines.

- The state Tax Code—Covers the state tax system for collection and enforcement of tax revenues and the associated laws.

- The U.S. Tax Code—The federal code that governs the collection of taxes by the IRS.

- The U.S. Title Code—A wide-sweeping document that governs many legislative actions for the entire U.S. government, including civil rights, law enforcement, and employment rights.

As with legal research issues, if you aren't comfortable with these books, get busy. Even if they don't all pertain to the type of law practiced in your office, you should at least know enough about each to speak knowledgeably should the subject come up. You should know how each book is laid out, how to find information under the various headings, and most importantly, when each code book applies and who uses it—judges, other attorneys, police officers, arbitrators, adjusters, executors, receivers, agents, etc.

Dealing with Physical Evidence

Few are the cases that don't have at least some kind of physical evidence associated with them. Personal injury cases involving car accidents offer a wealth of evidence, from materials left at the scene, to the physical conditions of the vehicles, drivers, and passengers, to photos, charts, diagrams, speed graphs, and evidence lists made by the investigators.

Slip and fall accidents can involve the shoes and clothing of the client, broken steps, loose tile, or any other uneven, rough, or broken surface that might have caused the accident.

Worker's compensation accidents take place in a myriad of different locations indoors and out, at various heights and depths, in all kinds of weather, and involving many kinds of equipment, machinery, chemicals, heat, cold, etc.

Criminal cases are filled with "instrumentalities" of the crime: knives, guns, tools, weapons, cars, etc., and "fruits" of the crime: money, drugs, property, etc. Each of these categories represents a certain type of evidence.

Business law cases are filled with paper-related evidence: reports, ledgers, checkbooks, charts, maps, graphs, blueprints, wills, trusts, contracts, codicils, etc.

If you have a case in your office that has the potential to go to court at some point, then everything is a potential exhibit: the client's files, the items someone collected at the scene of an accident or crime, the paperwork or documentation that proves or disproves something, and any physical item that the client, the witnesses, or the defendant can bring to court as proof of guilt, innocence, malfeasance, omissions, or errors.

The list of possible evidence is limited only by your imagination. You should treat every hard object—a broken tile, a defective brake pad, a file folder of accounting spreadsheets, etc.—as if it were the most valuable thing on earth. Your attorney may need to put that item on display in court one or even five years down the road. Store your physical evidence in a safe place, keep it dry, and protect it from any possible damage from too much handling by curious or untrained people. Sometimes your entire argument, e.g., that a product is defective, may rest on the condition of the physical evidence. Treat your evidence like gold regardless of its quantity, size, or relative importance.

To the untrained eye, physical evidence may not reveal much information. But what looks like a rusted piece of metal to you may reveal hundreds of interesting details to a mechanical engineer. The best way to handle evidence is not to. Go out and find expert help before you do anything. Some evidence may be delicate and may need special care to preserve it. Other evidence, like photos, videos, tape recordings, and handwriting exemplars should be reviewed by highly trained scientists who can determine authenticity, value, age, and other identifying characteristics for you.

If your firm represents the defendant in a case, your attorneys will file the appropriate discovery motions to get access to any physical evidence before the trial. Find some court-certified experts for your "hard" evidence—blood, firearms, photos, metal, fibers, wood, chemical products, etc.—and give them enough time to complete their study and prepare a report of their findings.

Better Legal Writing

As a wise old humorist once said, "Lawyers are the only people who can write a 10,000-word document and call it a 'brief.' "

One of the worst misconceptions of both attorneys and paralegals entering the legal field is that to be successful, everything they write must sound scholarly, legal, and tinged with the old-world Latin of their predecessors. This often misguided attempt to write like others in the legal profession usually leads to poor writing habits that create documents neither clients, judges, nor even other attorneys can understand.

Long-winded sentences, an array of complicated jargon, and a sea of passive voice prose only combine to cloud otherwise clear issues and confuse the reader. Unfortunately, the history of the legal profession has carved out this bad-writing model over a long period of time. Because legal writing has always been hard to understand, odd logic tells most attorneys and paralegals that there must be a good reason for it, so don't rock the boat by writing anything that even hints of clarity.

This is not to say that legal jargon has no place in the profession; it certainly applies to many situations. But the criteria for using complex jargon should be based on the answer to the question: Who is the reader?

If the reader is another legal professional, then it makes sense to use some familiar jargon to explain things to someone who already speaks that language. Problems arise when legal people write letters and reports to non-legal people. Because these readers don't travel in legal circles or understand these verbal shortcuts, the message is lost on them.

Any time you write an internal memo about a case to another attorney or paralegal, feel free to use jargon, abbreviations, and shortcuts that you know another legal professional will understand. This saves time for both of you and helps get the point across with a minimum of effort and paper.

However, any time you write something that goes outside the legal community—a letter, a report, a request for more information, a witness statement, etc.—you must avoid legal jargon whenever possible, especially when your audience may not understand your terminology.

Medical doctors, chiropractors, and scientific experts frequently make this mistake. Their reports are so filled with the terminology of their trades that the average attorney, insurance adjuster, hearing arbitrator, or judge will understand little of what is on the page. This inability to write for the reader irritates many people.

What follows is a way to improve the way you write by giving you some issues to think about before you pick up your pen or sit down in front of a typewriter or word processor. These suggestions will help you prepare your thoughts so you can write with less effort, more impact, and greater clarity. Take these tips and apply them to your legal writing projects: memos, memo briefs, case progress reports, client letters, representation letters, demand letters, settlement packages, etc.

Since you can't change the way the entire legal profession writes, see if you can improve the way *you* write for a start.

R.O.S.C.O.—A Model for Legal Writing Productivity

Sportswriter Red Smith once said, "There's nothing to writing. All you do is sit down at a typewriter and open a vein." This statement may accurately reflect the feelings of most legal professionals when it comes to putting words to paper.

Whether it's a one-page letter to an important client or a 50-page report to the senior partners in your firm, the process of business and legal writing often conjures up fear of failure feelings. This uneasiness can hover over the process of writing and interfere with your overall productivity. A critical client letter that needs to go out immediately may languish on the desk of a paralegal who doesn't know where or how to begin. Worse yet, if the person on the other end sees a jumbled, half-baked effort, what kind of impression does that convey about the paralegal writer or the law firm he or she supposedly represents?

Many people seem to think that good writing skills come from some kind of inherited talent, not from an actual process of skill-building. Nothing could be further from reality. True, good writers often seem blessed with a large and potent vocabulary and an ease of organization and expression, but these are acquired skills, just like those needed for interpreting legal matters, computer programming, accounting, or interviewing.

Good writers are made, not born. Powerful writing skills come from training, constant practice, and refinement, not from divine intervention.

It's a strange paradox that while most legal matters center around words, e.g., laws, rules, statutes, contracts, etc., legal writing is a subject that generally brings groans from paralegals.

"You want a memo covering the impact of our new client management filing system? By when?"

Faced with this assignment, what's the typical plan of attack? Usually, the person given this task gathers together a hodgepodge of material and sits down to work with no real idea of what to write in the beginning, middle, or end.

After a number of false starts, the writer may return a finished product that lacks clarity, power, or any semblance of organization. An important client letter may leave the office because of time deadlines or other case-related pressures, even if neither the paralegal nor the supervising attorney is fully satisfied with the work. Worse yet, the supervising attorney may not know how to offer appropriate suggestions to correct the problem.

Couple this with a lukewarm or even negative response by the reader on the other end, and you've seen the bad writing loop come full circle.

So what's the solution? Is there a way to organize a large or small legal writing project before you begin? Can you write with more confidence and clarity and better organize your thoughts? The answer is an unqualified "yes." Most good writing begins by following a few rules of organization. Let's start by reviewing a writing productivity model called R.O.S.C.O.

Used as a planning tool before each significant writing task, the R.O.S.C.O. model can help fill in the blanks before you pick up a pen or sit down at the keyboard. You also can use it as a training guide for any fellow employee having difficulty getting started. Remember that as a paralegal, the goal of your writing is not to "inform" but to get some action from your reader.

Complete each element of the R.O.S.C.O. model, which stands for *Reader*, *Outcome*, *Strategy*, *Content*, and *Organization*, and you'll see a logical progression starting to build. Answer the following questions before you start your next important legal writing project.

Reader

Who is the reader? A new client? A current client? The head adjuster for an insurance company? The opposing counsel? A staff member in another department? A friend? An enemy? The court clerk? The hearing judge on an important case? Knowing exactly who will read your message takes much of the guesswork out of writing.

What are his or her interests in the case? What about biases, opinions, or beliefs? What do you know about this person already? Do you have any pre-existing information or knowledge of your reader? Do you know his or her current position concerning the topic you're covering? Do you know of any biases or opinions that might require a delicate touch?

With these issues in mind, you can attempt to change your reader's mind, agree with or confirm his or her position, or provide useful information to improve his or her understanding of the problem at hand.

How does he or she feel about me or my firm? What information does your reader have about you or your law office? Is it a positive image, a negative image, or just neutral? Do you need to change your reader's mind about you or about the firm where you work?

Knowing your audience is critical to the success and survival of your message. Remember that your written material is competing with other written material.

Outcome

What do I want to accomplish by writing this? What is your ultimate goal? To continue an existing communication process? To start a new one? To relay some critical or timely information? To establish rapport? To settle a case? To express anger, neutrality, or excitement? Knowing what you want to accomplish before you start can take off much of the pressure.

What do I want the reader to do after reading this? What is the first thing you want him or her to do? Pick up the phone and call you? Settle the case? Lunge for his or her checkbook? Send it to another decision-maker? Act on it in the future? Refer you to an expert? Send you some more information?

Do I need to write anything at all? Is this piece of paper really necessary? Can you handle the matter with a phone call or a face-to-face meeting, or does it need documentation? Do you need to write something to protect you or your firm from potential malpractice problems later?

Make sure your message is strong enough to fight its way to the top of your reader's attention zone. Don't just add another piece to the vast paper shuffle.

Strategy

Of each of the R.O.S.C.O. elements, the *Strategy* aspect is probably the most flexible. You can go in an infinite number of directions to get your point across with clarity, impact, and style.

What overall approach should I use? Choose the best way to get your point across. Pick an approach that's the most feasible, cost-effective, and time-productive. Follow the old tongue-twisting advertising slogan: "Tell them what you're going to say, say what you're going to say, and tell them what you just said."

Which tone will work best? You have a wide range of options to choose from: hard, easy, friendly, legal, warm, cool, dramatic, subtle, bold, direct, or indirect. Choose the best one to get your message across in a notable manner.

How formal or informal shall I make it? It helps to know in advance if your reader is a friend, an acquaintance, an enemy, or a stranger. With this information, you can accurately guess how your reader will perceive you and your message. A friendly, low-key approach might work best, or you may need to add some stern language to make your point.

Content

This next element of the R.O.S.C.O. model refers to the "meat-and-potatoes" of your message, i.e., what you plan to say and how you plan to say it.

What information do I need to convey? Give your reader enough information to stimulate some action on his or her part. Explain whatever is necessary to achieve your outcome. Help your reader learn more than he or she already knows. Gather the available case material to include if it's necessary.

How much information will serve my objectives? Choose a logical midpoint between too much and too little. Decide if you need to provide additional data from the case file like reports, depositions, statements, photos, video, charts, graphs, maps, reports, or briefs.

How much detail do I need to include? Try to break each part of your message down into individual sections so as not to overwhelm your reader with information. Decide between too much detail and not giving him or her enough to make an intelligent or immediate decision. Brevity is usually more effective than length.

Organization

Finally, the last element of the R.O.S.C.O. model deals with the physical presentation of your message—what the reader actually holds in his or her hands.

How should I organize the information? Carefully choose the physical layout of your written message. You may be able to cover it with a one-page letter or it may take five. You may need to include a number of attachments, additional information sent under separate cover, a spiral-bound report, deposition copies, a video tape, or even a stamped return envelope or a reply card. Make it easy for your reader to go from top to bottom and make an appropriate, timely reply.

What items should come first? Last? Give some careful thought to the flow of the piece. You might want to put the good news in front and the bad news at the end or buried in the middle. If it's a settlement letter, be sure to include all of the necessary information to help the reader make a decision and then ask for a response by a specific date.

Decide if you can use a direct lead, which gives the reader your news or information right away, or an indirect lead, which delays the message until a bit later on.

How should I arrange the information to support my ideas? You may want to use "bullets," numbered points, or an outline format to highlight your main ideas. You might provide a brief overview at the opening, followed by a description of each point. If the reader will need to refer to other pages, choose a format—parentheses, footnotes, etc.—that's easy to read and use. Choose a format that encourages the reader to act after reviewing your information.

Each of the five factors that make up the R.O.S.C.O. model serves a distinct purpose. The five factors offer guidelines to help you get started. Once you know the answers to these questions, you can begin to write with more confidence. Instead of your thrashing around with only a vague idea of your ultimate goal, the R.O.S.C.O. model can get you going in the right direction. It's not a cure-all for every writing problem but, rather, a springboard you can use to begin your writing tasks.

You probably won't need to use the model if you're just dashing off a quick note, memo, or fax, but you should definitely consider it for your next high-priority, high-value letter, brief, or settlement offer.

When you know your audience and what you want from them, as well as your strategy to reach that audience, the words will come with less exertion. And that *is* the key to effective legal writing, legal research, and case management—creating a quality product with a minimum of hardship and effort.

six

FINDING THE PLAYERS: How to Locate Witnesses, Defendants, and Lost Clients

"For purposes of action, nothing is more useful than narrowness of thought combined with energy of will."—Henri Frederic Amiel

*C*onsider the three disturbing scenarios that follow:

1. You've just completed the initial phases of your client's big-money personal injury car-accident case. You've verified the insurance from the other driver, taken care of the client's property damage, sent the client to a doctor for treatment, and reviewed the police report carefully.

   Late one Friday, you have a very brief conversation with the only witness to the crash who tells you he is just going out the door and asks if he can get back to you on Monday. You dutifully leave him your office number and, when Monday and Tuesday come and go, you call him back. A metallic voice answers the phone with this chilling phrase: "The number you have reached is no longer in service. Please hang up and try your call again."

   Your star witness, the one person who can verify your client's side of the story, has moved.

2. Your partnership dissolution case has dragged on for months and months. Both partners hate each other and have disrupted depositions, ruined settlement meetings, and generally made everyone's life miserable. After months of waiting for his partner to cooperate, the client says he's tired of negotiating and wants the courts to settle this business "divorce." The defendant, a 20-year resident of the community, fails to show up at his office on the day your process server comes with the summons and complaint. Not only is he not there, but his furniture, file cabinets, and telephones are also missing.

3. Your firm has really worked hard on this probate case—long hours, bad takeout food, no rest for weeks and weeks. You've finally come to the end of a long road that started nearly two years ago. The estate money coming to the client represents a tidy sum. Your firm's percentage of the total check will make the partners happy for quite a spell.

The client is kind of a maverick, changing jobs and cities often enough to have a standing account with a moving and storage firm. You just spoke with her a few months ago to give her an update on the case. With the check in hand you send off a letter saying, "We've settled the case. Please call us immediately to get your check."

After a week, your letter comes back marked, "Return to Sender—No Forwarding Address." The client's check sits in your firm's trust account, gathering dust.

So what two things do these minor tragedies have in common? A strong sense of disappointment and a renewed feeling that the "real" work in the case has just begun. We all like to feel good about our work. These new problems locating witnesses, defendants, and clients can only add to your frustration level. Just when you think the case has turned the corner toward settlement or you've even received the money from the other side, you can't enjoy any sense of accomplishment or closure. What do you do now that your case is in apparent shambles? How do you cope with missing participants? When all appears bleak, keep the following rules in mind.

Plan for these surprises before they happen: While no one expects you to have a crystal ball attached to your desk, you may be able to anticipate and ward off some problems with your witnesses, defendants, and clients.

Don't be shy about asking your witnesses if they plan to move anytime soon or if they will change jobs, addresses, or phone numbers in the near future. When you send them a "sign under penalty of perjury" statement, have them include their driver's licenses and Social Security numbers with their signatures.

Keep track of any available information that might help you later if they disappear: home and work addresses; home and work phone numbers; wives', husbands', in-laws', or childrens' names; license plates; post office box numbers; rental property addresses; probation or parole officers' or military base supervisors' names; bank accounts or finance company addresses; etc.

Try to make some assumptions about where these people might be in three months, six months, or a year from now. Are your witnesses, defendants, or clients in jail right now? In the military? In a community college or state university study program? Enrolled in a trade school or technical school? Married with a new last name? Divorced and using a previous name?

Find out where they work and make a note of their work supervisors' names and phone numbers if you can. This information may help you if these people quit, get transferred to another division in the same company, or change jobs but stay in the same career field.

Learn to read the clues of movement: impending address, job, or marital status changes. If you're really concerned a witness, defendant, or client will skip out on you, make a note on your calendar to review the file at appropriate intervals, checking status and verifying any new information.

Don't worry more than necessary about these delays: Accept the fact that there are some people who will not cooperate under any circumstances. Some fail to cooperate no matter how nice you are; others are negative and uncooperative even if you threaten them with civil, legal, or financial punishments. Remember that we live in a mobile, ever-changing society. People move from job to job and to different cities, states, or even countries much more readily than they did 20 years ago.

We also live in a highly transient country. A surprisingly large portion of our population has no real community roots and seems to drift from town to town, working and living just day to day. Many of these same people who bounce around like this also need more legal services—for accidents, insurance claims, arrests, etc.—than more structured, longtime community residents.

Don't lose sleep over what you cannot control or couldn't have foreseen. Regardless of what the attorneys or other related case participants say, it's not the end of the world. There are always other ways to proceed even though it seems as if everyone who is important to your case is gone. In these apparent last-resort situations, you can rely on taped conversations for missing witnesses, sub-service or service by publication for your missing defendants, and due-diligence court orders to get your share of client settlement fees.

Focus your attention and energies on more positive outcomes: finding these people and successfully closing the case. Concentrate on which people you need to find, when you need to find them, where, how, and why. You'll need to budget some of your time, an investigator's time, and most likely some money from your firm's expense account.

Start looking immediately for your missing person: In most cases, time is of the essence. Don't waste a single minute floundering around for more information, motivation, or a place to start. If you wait too long to start the chase, you'll get far behind and fall into the "You just missed him" trap.

As soon as you hear of or recognize a potential problem, get busy. Pick up the phone, call your firm's outside investigators, and give them all the information they'll need to start a "skip trace."

Try not to waste time tracking undeliverable certified letters or disconnected phone numbers. Focus your efforts on postal checks, telephone directory assistance, credit and property searches, and places of employment first. These areas usually offer the best results in the least amount of time.

Use a checklist each time you search for missing people: Create a checklist of skip trace and locate activities for missing persons. Make copies and add them to your problem case files. Using the checklist ensures you won't forget any critical steps or leave out any important information that may become useful later. It also keeps you from covering old ground and wasting time tracking dead end leads.

Late in this chapter, you will find a checklist you can use for your own cases.

Be prepared to wait for results: Witnesses, defendants, and clients can disappear and reappear as if by magic. One day, after you've abandoned all hope, your long-lost client will miraculously phone your office to ask, "Whatever happened with my case?"

Finding missing people takes equal portions of skill and patience, but it also requires a fair amount of plain old luck. You may stumble across a piece of information that solves the entire mystery, or you may get a call from the missing person out of the blue. You may just have to resign yourself to the fact that all you can do is all you can do and wait for something to happen. If you apply proven search methods and invest some time and patience in the waiting game, you may be rewarded with the people or information you seek.

Putting Investigators on the Trail

The decision to use investigators to locate missing persons depends on a few important factors: the cost considerations, the overall strength and importance of the case, and time deadlines. If the case is relatively minor in terms of dollar values, or the participation of a missing witness is less consequential to the outcome, it probably makes better sense to save the money an investigator would require to locate the person. It's pointless to spend a large sum to find someone who might not contribute much to the case. If you have other witnesses or more viable options at your disposal, there's no need to throw good money after bad.

However, if time pressures are suddenly looming, it makes excellent sense to get investigators busy on the case. They can often get good results in as little as one day or even one hour. Using their resources, some of which are more nefarious than others, they can often track down someone in such a short period of time that it saves the case and more than justifies their fees.

Always remember that no matter how much you like working with your investigators or how well you get along with them on a professional level, it's still a business for them and for you. They'll know from the tone of your voice or the urgency of your notes when a skip trace or locate is a "rush" and thereby commands higher fees for faster work. Be prepared to pay more for someone you need to find by yesterday.

Investigator Joe Coyle, from Joe Coyle and Associates in San Diego, California, offers more advice for paralegals who need to find missing people: "My clients usually contact me after the local marshal's office or an attorney service has failed to locate the party who needs to be found or served. Sometimes the address listed as 'bad' by these services is actually good, so I can save your firm some time and money. More often, however, the person has indeed moved. Many of these people fail to notify the Department of Motor Vehicles or the U.S. Postal Service of their new address so the search becomes much more difficult."

Coyle has seen a number of cases in which the paralegals could have solved the problems themselves with a bit more work. "The biggest mistake I see paralegals make is their failure to do a little research on their own before calling me. Sometimes simply looking in the phone book or calling Directory Assistance will help them locate the person. By doing a few simple checks on their own, they can save their firm and the client hundreds of dollars in investigator fees."

Coyle cautions, "When the person has dropped out of sight or doesn't wish to be found, you shouldn't hesitate to call a professional investigator. Always remember that the clock is ticking. The longer you wait before you give the case to someone like me, the colder the leads may become. This just makes it harder and more expensive to find the person."

If you do decide to hire investigators to locate missing people, make sure you give them all of the information you have. "The next biggest mistake," says Coyle, "is that attorneys and paralegals fail to give me enough usable information about the person. Sometimes a paralegal will send me a package of legal papers to serve or give me an assignment to locate and interview a lost witness. I may get the name and maybe an address, but nothing else. It's hard to do much with such scant information. These kinds of locates can become very expensive, if they are possible at all.

"When I'm talking with attorneys or paralegals about a case, I emphasize the importance of providing as much information as they have about the person we're looking for. I ask them to let me read the entire file, and I find out if they have any other information that's not in the file. Dates of birth, Social Security numbers, driver's license numbers, vehicle information, names of relatives and employers, and even the actual circumstances of the case can really help me narrow my search."

Investigators can never have *too* much information to go on. "Don't try to put me on a case with nothing more than a telephone call," he warns. "For accountability purposes, it's extremely important to have a letter or some document that clearly spells out what I'm being retained to do or what service I'm being asked to provide."

In light of recent tragedies involving the unauthorized use of names and addresses of television and movie actors, the laws concerning the release of personal information have really become quite strict.

"In California," says Coyle, "private investigators may get access to Department of Motor Vehicles records for the purposes of getting residence address information in order to serve legal papers. Any investigator who wants to use this system ethically must post a large bond, pay various fees, and maintain a 'log' with a case number or a copy of the file to prove that the records inquiry was made for the stated, legal purpose. A copy of the summons alone isn't good enough. I usually ask for a letter from the attorney specifically assigning me to locate and serve 'the attached summons and complaint to the below named defendant.' I know it's extra work for my clients, but it protects all of us from malpractice claims later on."

While he realizes how important and critical some cases can be for an entire law office, Coyle stands firm on his professional ethics. He won't sacrifice his career just to find a missing person.

"I won't do anything illegal or unethical. I don't know how many times I've heard someone say, 'You can't be a good investigator without bending the rules a little.' There's a big difference between bending rules and breaking laws. Some investigators, either through ignorance of the law or overzealousness, choose to break the law now and then just to solve a case, gain access to information, and keep their attorney clients happy. I've heard this behavior can range from accessing certain databases under false pretenses all the way to installing illegal wiretaps.

"When attorneys, paralegals, and investigators choose to break the law or abuse the system and get caught, the whole legal profession suffers a setback. Everyone else's job gets tougher as a result."

Using an investigator is a choice you must make after you weigh the factors surrounding the case. Coyle says it's always better to be too prepared for a possible court trial than not prepared at all. You can never know too much about the case.

"Don't ever be afraid to ask your investigator for help," he says, "or for some suggestions as to the best way to proceed on a case. An experienced investigator can be a great resource. Many investigators working today are armed with college degrees and lots of street savvy instead of a .38-caliber and some shoe leather. Don't 'wing it' alone. Use the resources of a good investigator when necessary."

Following the Trail Yourself

As investigator Joe Coyle mentioned, the more you can do on your own, the better chance you have of finding the person without outside help. Your efforts to start the search process first can save time for you and money for your firm.

Remember the examples that opened this chapter. Each one presents a different case problem and a different type of missing person. These examples may be very similar to cases you're working on right now or to ones that may come up later. Try not to get discouraged as you search and wait. Keep your mind fixed on the various incentives that will come when you locate a missing person: financial rewards for your clients and your firm; legal and professional satisfaction for finding the people in time to meet case deadlines, depositions, and court hearings; and most importantly, additional job satisfaction for you.

To find these lost people, follow some simple and inexpensive step-by-step procedures first, before you move on to other techniques or get help from an investigator.

Help from the Phone Company

Hearing the recorded voice of a phone company employee tell you an important phone number is no longer in service can chill your bones. But although it may appear that the person has moved, don't jump to any immediate conclusions. Consider first that there may be troubles with the phone line. Try your calls at different times later in the day, and maybe the phone lines will work again.

Perhaps the phone was in fact disconnected, but the resident still lives at that address. Some people have problems paying their bills and can't get phone service. Sending your investigator or, if you have enough time, a certified letter to the address may get an immediate response.

If you're sure the person no longer lives at the address, wait a few more days to see if he or she gave a forwarding number to the telephone company that wasn't immediately installed on the old number.

If neither of these tactics works, turn to the phone company itself. It offers one of the most inexpensive skip trace services in the country. Dial Directory Assistance at 411 or 555-1212 (whichever works for your particular calling area) and ask for a new listing for this person. Be sure to ask for an address too. If you're looking for Mr. Randy Jones, have the operator give you all of the R. Jones listings.

Using your copy of the most current phone book, look for the person's name and all abbreviations of his or her first name. If you know the spouse's, relatives', or in-laws' names, look for those too. It never hurts to call and ask; they may lead you to the person you want. If the surname is not common, you might try calling straight down the column. After years of fielding misdirected phone calls, many people learn to identify and locate unrelated persons who share their last name.

If by chance you know your missing person has moved to another state, start with the area code and Directory Assistance (555-1212) again. Get an atlas or a map of the state and find the city. Go to the phone book and get the area code. If the state uses one area code for complete coverage, ask the operator to check for the new listing statewide. (They don't always like to do this, so ask nicely.) You'd be amazed how many times this works.

If you have the phone numbers of other witnesses, call and ask if they know the person you're looking for. In some cases, the witnesses will have been passengers in the same car, friends together at the scene of an incident, or otherwise acquainted by virtue of professional or personal relationships.

Help from Property Records

You can try to find out if your missing person owns property in one of two ways: by checking the county property lists or by getting the information from a private real estate database service. The first method involves a trip to the county hall of records or courthouse for a detailed search under the person's name. You also can do some of your research at the county assessor's office to see where the person's property tax bills are being sent.

The database method is much faster, although it can be expensive. With most of these services, the on-line time is charged by the minute plus a standard search fee. Many private investigators subscribe to these real estate search services and can get this information for you.

Keep in mind this property search method only works if the

missing person's name is on the deed or title to a piece of property; it doesn't locate renters, just owners.

Help from the Motor Vehicles Department

Nearly everyone over the age of 16 in this country has a driver's license, a state identification card, or a car registered in his or her name.

Many investigation firms subscribe to data search companies that are allowed access to state motor vehicle records. Privacy of information laws vary from state to state, with some quite liberal and others, like California's, much more stringent. Depending on your particular state, you can get DMV information that ranges from extremely helpful to barely useful.

The key to the value of DMV information relates mostly to its recency. DMV records, unlike fine wines, don't get better with age. Old addresses, bad license plates, and other similar dated information can only cause you or your investigator to waste valuable searching time. Most people are basically honest, and they notify their DMV soon after they move. This keeps them current in the computer files and helps them get their new registration tags and license renewals. It's fairly simple and painless to locate these people. However, there are some people who don't notify DMV after each move either because they're forgetful, or have crime on their minds, or they move so often that they have a hard time keeping track of themselves.

Many state DMV records are cross-referenced, meaning that entering the person's name also will give you his or her driver's license number, driving record and license history, and any vehicles—including boats, trailers, and motor homes—that are registered under his or her name. Depending on who gets the information for you and the speed of your state DMV office, it usually takes about 10 working days to get a printout copy of someone's driving record.

If you run into roadblocks with one name, try running same-surnamed relatives or children if you know of them.

You can often verify that the information is current by checking the last date the DMV interacted with the person. Anything over one year old is probably suspect. If your information is fairly current, it's much more likely to be accurate.

Help from Credit Agencies

If your firm or your investigators have access to one of the "Big Three" credit record services—Trans-Union, CBI/Equifax, or TRW—you may be able to locate a missing person by entering his or her Social Security number into these credit history databases. The credit report should list the most recent address. While the state DMV may be a bit behind with good address information, rest assured that these credit report agencies will do their best to have a current address because their credit card customers (the banks, Visa, Mastercard, gas companies, department stores, etc.) want their money from their cardholders.

Many fraudulent people use several different Social Security numbers to confuse creditors and keep the IRS and other agencies off their backs. If you find several names and several numbers, you may have a more serious criminal violator on your hands.

Besides providing location and credit status, the credit report is useful for gauging a person's assets should a civil suit become necessary. Besides acting as a first-look net worth indicator, the report also may list court judgements against the person, wage attachments, and state and federal tax liens. This information can help you plan your case better and may offer other suggestions to help find the person.

If your firm doesn't subscribe to a database information service, you might want to do some research and present a list of these companies to your attorneys. Many of these firms offer a wide range of information, including DMV records; personal and business credit; property, title, and asset searches; and criminal, civil, and judicial index records.

If you do decide to use one of these services, help it as you would an investigator by providing as much information as possible.

Help from the U.S. Postal Service

In his gripping sociological study of law enforcement, *City Police*, author Jonathan Rubinstein spent several months riding with the Philadelphia Police Department. One day he was sitting in a patrol car with a veteran officer. As they watched people pass on the street, the cop pointed to a man walking near a row of houses and said, "See that guy? If I knew what he does about the people here I'd be the best cop in the district. I been here twelve years and I don't know what he knows. And I know more than most."

The Philadelphia officer was referring to the postman, walking from house to business, delivering the mail. The USPS can help you find missing people because its own "army" of letter carriers and postal workers delivers mail to literally everyone old enough to reach a mailbox.

Suppose your defendant gives only a post office box as an address. So how do you serve him? Thanks to some help from the U.S. Postal Service, your firm's process server can get access to P.O. Box subscriber information. Armed with a civil process, a process server can request the physical address of a Post Office Box holder. Under federal law, the Postmaster at the box location has to release the information to a registered process server needing to serve an individual. Using this fast and inexpensive method, you can learn the street address of your defendant.

Another tremendously simple technique requires only that you send a letter to the missing person's old address with the phrase "Address Correction Requested—Return Postage Guaranteed" across the front of the envelope. This trick will often give you the person's new forwarding address, all for only the cost of a few stamps.

Help from the Government

Whether you like it or not, our government keeps tabs on everybody, young or old, large or small. Banks of federal computers whir and grind 24 hours a day, keeping track of us for tax purposes and reasons of business, national security, defense, law enforcement, property, voting, mail, health, farming, industry, and for a range of other reasons we're not always too sure about.

While much of this information is protected at the federal, state, county, and city level, some of it is not. With a little diligence and some careful searching, you can find out many things about a person. Your tax dollars have paid for this tracking system, it's legal and relatively accurate and efficient, so why not put it to good use for your firm?

Here's a short list of some of the offices, divisions, and databanks within our vast government where you can do some research:

At the County Courthouse/Hall of Records:

Fictitious business license applications: You can search the files for addresses here by the person's name or by the company's fictitious business name.

Marriage, birth, death certificates: Access to these records may give you new leads or answer questions about the whereabouts of a missing person.

Criminal cases: Using the public records of Municipal and Superior Court proceedings, you can identify convicted criminals and find out if they are in jail, on parole, or on probation.

Civil cases: You can research civil court cases and locate plaintiffs and defendants involved in past proceedings.

Other Resources:

The Office of the Secretary of State in your state: You can call this office in your state capitol to request address and personnel information, such as the agent for service, for a corporation incorporated or doing business in your state.

Marshals, constables, sheriffs as process servers: You can contract with these public officials to serve your civil process papers for you. They are often more efficient and less expensive than private enterprise attorney services. These law enforcement officials are especially helpful if you have defendants to serve in small towns and rural areas.

I remember handling a case for an attorney who required me to find and serve a defendant in a small Tennessee town. I found the person, but his address was listed as the local post office. I called and spoke with one of the sheriff's deputies who worked the area. He immediately recognized the defendant's name and his real home address (at the end of a dead-end dirt road). I sent him the required fees for civil process service and the summons and complaint. He served the defendant and mailed back the proof of service for filing in less than one week.

Depositions, Dollars, and Due Diligence

Sometimes you want to find missing people, like clients, to give them money. Other times you may want to find and depose witnesses and other case participants to get critical information. And still other times you may want to find and serve defendants for the purposes of relieving them of their money. In each case, make sure you use the right piece of paper for the job. If you have to subpoena witnesses, tell them what to bring with them (as with a *subpoena duces tecum*), when to appear, and how much, if anything, they will be paid for their time.

Lastly, if you or your investigator decides to throw in the towel and give up trying to find someone, make sure you document every effort to both locate and serve the person. Due diligence laws vary from state to state. If you fail to follow correct "sub-service" or service-by-publication requirements, you could run into many proof-of-service headaches later on.

Some states require at least three bona fide attempts to serve a person and three different types of records checks, i.e., voter registration rolls, DMV records, and a postal check, before you can serve by publication or any other similar legal method. Do what you can to find the person and then move on to other cases.

Missing Person Search Checklist

Here's a detailed checklist you can copy as one of your case file forms when you need to find your missing witnesses, defendants, and clients. Type the items on a page and put a line next to each one, so you can check it off as you complete it. Many investigators use a similar form themselves.

Current Phone Book Listing
Citywide Telephone Directory Assistance
Statewide Directory Assistance
Call other witnesses/family members/workplaces

Property Search
County Property Tax Records
Deeds and Titles

DMV Records By Name
DMV Records By Vehicle
DMV Records By Boat/Other Vehicles
Out-of-State DMV Records Check

Credit History—Personal and Business
Social Security Number Check

Postal Check
Voter Registration

Civil Index—Superior and Municipal Courts
Federal Civil Index
City, State, and Federal Criminal Cases

Fictitious Business Names
City Business License
Special Licenses/Permits/Degrees

Secretary of State Incorporations

City Business Tax Liens
State Tax Liens
Federal Tax Liens

Birth/Marriage/Death Records

Most people, unless they are wanted fugitives, leave some paper trail behind them. To locate various witnesses, defendants, or forgetful clients, just use the resources at your disposal along with a little common sense.

Get authorization to make important decisions before you proceed. Keep time and deadline pressures, dollar figures, degrees of difficulty, and your firm's and client's spending limits in mind at all times. Do what you can on your own, then get the help of a licensed, qualified investigator after you've exhausted the possibilities on your end.

Rest assured that your attorneys don't expect you to become a PI nor should you want to be one if you're comfortable working as a paralegal. Do what you can from your desk and make a few trips to some governmental agencies for more help. Otherwise, stick to your own job and rely on skip trace and locate experts to do the leg work for you. This helps you avoid any conflicts of interest, malpractice, or other legal or statutory violations.

Don't forget that when trying to find missing persons, luck and patience often play just as important a part as skill and experience.

seven

EXPANDING THE JOB: Other Things You Will Do

"Since we cannot know all that is to be known of everything, we ought to know a little about everything."—Blaise Pascal

*T*he paralegal profession is evolving rapidly. The way attorneys perceive paralegals has changed for the better. And the way attorneys use paralegals has changed for the better as well. Gone are the days when a paralegal was hired to be a glorified secretary with some legal research skills. Today's paralegals are actively involved in many facets of the law office operation, no matter what the specialty.

Recent employment studies relating to the paralegal profession offer some interesting statistics. According to one survey, about 60 percent of this nation's paralegals work in private-practice law firms, small, mid-size, and large; 10 percent work for the government, at either the local, state, or federal level; another 10 percent work in corporations, banks, insurance companies, and financial institutions; and the remaining 20 percent work for legal aid groups, political lobbies, trade unions, special interest groups, private businesses, and in their own paralegal practices that offer limited legal advice and services to the general public.

Independent Paralegals

The reference to paralegals with their own practices may light your eyes with thoughts of private enterprise and "being your own boss." However, be aware that self-employment for paralegals is a very limited option. In most states, any activity by a paralegal must be performed under the systematic supervision and control of an attorney; self-directed activity is termed "unauthorized practice of law," which is subject to prosecution.

A few states do permit a certain autonomy to paralegals. In these states, paralegals may perform routine legal services for clients—preparing documents, conducting inventories for estates, filling out forms, notarizing papers, and making filings with courts or administrative bodies—so long as they do not give legal advice. In some states, independent paralegals may offer their services to attorneys. In these cases, the paralegals operate their own businesses but do indeed perform their work under supervision. Independent paralegals tend to be highly experienced and to have developed expertise in narrow, specialized aspects of the field.

Still one more arena of autonomy open to some paralegals in some areas is as "enrolled agents." The designation "enrolled agent" is not an entry-level title. The seasoned paralegal must undergo specialized training and generally some certification process as well. An enrolled agent may actually represent clients in administrative hearings before certain agencies such as the Internal Revenue Service or a worker's compensation board.

The numbers I have cited indicate that most paralegals are employed by law firms ranging widely in size. The same breakdown of paralegal employment illustrates the inherent flexibility of the profession as a whole. Few careers offer the chance to work for so many different entities—from the private sector to the government to social and community service organizations—all within the same framework that makes up the vast legal field. This flexibility brings more choices with it; different types of paralegals can do different things, based upon their education, training, work experience, and career goals.

While most paralegals know a little bit about a great many legal topics, e.g., civil litigation, contracts, business and corporate law, wills, trusts and estates, etc., some know a great deal about one specific area of the law. These paralegal specialists differ from their counterparts by virtue of their extensive knowledge and experience pertaining to a certain legal subject.

In some progressive firms, paralegal specialists have been given a great deal of autonomy to handle client relations and case management. These paralegals spend much of their time meeting with new clients, explaining various legal procedures to them, and tracking the progress of each case from start to settlement. More recently, qualified paralegals have taken on a new role: They serve as the clients' "go-between" with the attorneys, updating both parties as the case progresses.

In other instances, veteran paralegals have played a significant role in preparing cases for trial. The scope of their use has grown exponentially as their knowledge of the law and courtroom procedures has increased.

Paralegals today help attorneys do nearly everything except actually try the case in court. By assisting with legal research, drafting preliminary briefs, recording witness statements, cataloging evidence, preparing interrogatories and tracking their return, and helping with witness lists, discovery motions, and appeals, today's paralegals take on more responsibility for the success of their attorneys' court cases than ever before.

Instead of doing simple research and making telephone calls, paralegals in many firms are cross-trained to take a case from its initial inception stages all the way through to the end. Here, the attorneys merely monitor the progress of the case, stepping in to offer guidance, file appropriate motions, appear in court, or meet with the clients or opposing counsel to settle the case.

Still other paralegals are becoming quite skilled as negotiators. Since much of the work surrounding business law, contracts, real estate, and insurance-related cases involves the typical back-and-forth haggling over dollar figures, paralegals are entering this stimulating, action-packed arena with more confidence than ever before.

Many of these tough negotiators started small, settling relatively low-dollar cases under the guidance of an attorney. As their experience and confidence grew, they began to get more involved with high-level, big-money negotiations, working closely with an attorney battling the other side.

In some offices, the senior paralegal will take control of a case as it is reaching the settlement stage. This person will contact the adjuster, opposing counsel, or other similar party, submitting demand packages and beginning to make offers and counter-offers as necessary. Obviously, many years of training and experience are prerequisite to a paralegal's attaining this level of responsibility.

Some paralegals spend time preparing clients for litigation; some get involved in negotiations; some go to government offices to pick up documents or to courthouses to file papers; and some even answer calendar calls for their attorneys. But the great majority of paralegals spend the bulk of their time handling paper-work—research, writing, indexing, and proofreading.

Research

The nature of the practice determines the nature of the research. In general, paralegals do factual research and write up factual memoranda, then turn over the fruits of their labor to attorneys for interpretation.

Research takes many forms. At the discovery phase of litigation, paralegals may play an important role, checking up on laws to find what is discoverable. They search laws and precedents to learn what types of documents it is permissible to request from the opposing side. Paralegals who have been granted the necessary autonomy may then contact attorneys for the opposing party and request document production. They may have to justify their requests with details of the laws that they have searched. When the documents come in, paralegals may join with attorneys in checking the submitted documents for completeness. They may categorize and index the documents. They may even read, analyze, and summarize some of the less complex documents. Another task of the paralegal is to set up the documents and their information on a database in a modern, automated office. In fact, paralegals remain active in the discovery phase right up to interpretation of the documents. Then attorneys take over and relate the facts to laws and precedents.

A supervising attorney may also ask a paralegal to do some initial research at the earliest stages of preparing a matter, or later on as the attorney marshals a plan toward winning the case. This research may be conducted in law libraries, in public libraries, or sitting at a computer using a WESTLAW® or LEXIS® program.

If you have taken a paralegal training program—and more and more paralegals are undergoing formal classroom training—you will have received instruction in the use of various legal research tools and methods of legal research. If you come to a paralegal position without formal training, the firm will give you more limited training with the books and journals it uses and the computer programs to which it subscribes. This more narrow training limits your initiative in researching other sources. On the other hand, it may well whet your appetite to go further by enrolling in in-service courses or in a paralegal training program.

As a paralegal, you are never expected to work entirely alone. You are not required to know the law nor to act as a lawyer. Orientation, guidance, and direction will steer you toward the methods that are accepted in your office.

Legal research can be fascinating. It may involve consulting indexes that send you to books and journals. It can lead you to secondary authorities that define terms and give you an overall picture of the legal issues involved. The secondary authorities offer commentaries, restatements of laws, and the very latest legal philosophical thought. The secondary authorities in turn can steer you towards the proper primary authorities: constitutions, statutes, judicial cases, rules of court, and administrative decisions and regulations. Finally, you must "shepardize"®, that is, follow the subsequent history of the laws and cases to be certain that decisions have not been overturned, that the law which you uncovered is still "good law."

There is a vast array of resources from which you may draw your legal research. At the earliest stages of your career, you will begin using only a few. As your skills and expertise mature, you will probably expand the number of tools you use. The nature of the practice

also will determine the nature of the research. In some types of matters—personal injury, medical malpractice, or product liability, for
instance—you might find yourself consulting medical journals, popular magazines, or newspaper clipping files as well as the more tradi-
tional legal sources.

Much of orthodox legal research involves following up on cross-
references. Thus, as you read a case report you find that footnotes
refer you to constitutional verities, to various laws and rulings, and
to other cases. Law review articles and legal newspapers and journals
may also send you to many other sources by way of footnotes. You
will need a firm grasp of the "Uniform System of Citation" in order
to follow the footnotes to their sources and to zero in on the appropriate pages.

The same "Uniform System of Citation," also known as the "Blue
Book," will serve as your guide in writing citations when you are
called upon to draft preliminary briefs. And the Blue Book will be
your standard when you proofread completed manuscripts or documents for accuracy of citations and proper form. The Blue Book is a
worthwhile sourcebook for you to purchase for your own reference
and for private study at home. You can buy this inexpensive book in
any law school bookstore.

The citation form in the Blue Book will not help you when you
consult print indexes, computer indexes, or *Shepard's Citations*. Each
index has its own system, and *Shepard's* has a detailed codification
method all its own. The front pages of print indexes or citators and
the first few screens of their computer counterparts give detailed instructions for their use. Shepard's/McGraw-Hill publishes an entire
booklet entitled *How To Use SHEPARD'S CITATIONS*. Learning to
use any of these is not a do-it-yourself project, but once you have
received instruction and have gotten some practice, you can become
a pro.

The indexes and citators are only finding tools. You must follow
through by going to the sources to check for yourself whether or not
the specific laws are relevant and whether the facts of the cases cited
are "on point" or peripherally related to the facts of the case you
are researching. Case reporters include a syllabus—which is a brief
description of the facts, issues, and resolution of the case and carry

the full decision. As a non-lawyer you will not be making the final determination, but you can be extremely useful to your attorneys by eliminating irrelevant rulings and decisions, in highlighting the most likely precedents, and in listing and possibly summarizing the cases to which they should direct their attention.

You will probably find it useful to do your research at both print sources and major computer sources, either WESTLAW or LEXIS. The computer sources are often quicker to use and, in some cases, more up-to-date than print sources. The print sources may be more complete and almost certainly go back further in time, giving better background and history. Some sources include constitutions, statutes, administrative materials, rules of court, digests, case reports of various jurisdictions, law reviews and law journals, legal newspapers, case report updates, restatements, and looseleaf services. This somewhat daunting list need not be overwhelming. You will learn to use these sources one at a time in their relation to specific research. As you look over the list of what you will eventually need to learn how to use, you can readily recognize that a paralegal is indeed a professional and that the position of paralegal is a career position and not just a job.

Other vital paperwork/research in which many paralegals are involved is cite checking. Cite checking is especially important on appellate briefs. The cite checker goes through the brief, to the indexes, and even the laws and casebooks themselves, to be certain that each case is accurately cited. Deciding whether or not the case cited actually is relevant and proves a point is the domain of the attorneys. However, determining that the source is accurately described, that the citation is in approved style and form, and that all numbers are accurate (watch for transpositions of digits) is often the assignment of the paralegal. The paralegal must be certain that the brief is ready for presentation and must alert the attorney to any potential problems in the body of the brief or in the cases cited.

And finally there is shepardizing. Some very large law firms reserve shepardizing for their young associates because it is so important. Other equally large law firms turn this crucial task over to paralegals. Shepardizing is the last step before trial. It involves consulting *Shepard's Citations* to identify all references to the statute, constitutional point, or landmark case that your attorney is citing as authority. The purpose of the shepardizing search is to be certain that the precedent has not been overturned, and that it is still a good and valid law. Notation in a Shepard's Citator indicates at a glance if there is any question. The letter "o" appears before a reference if the precedent was overruled in any way. The person doing the shepardizing can refer directly to those cases preceded by an "o." A quick glance at the syllabus should indicate whether the entire ruling was upturned or whether the precedent did not hold because of a matter of fact. Then a comparison of the facts of the current case and the case cited by *Shepard's* can guide your attorney as he or she goes off to court. Just think of how embarrassing it would be for your attorney to cite a law or precedent that no longer is valid!

Writing

Paralegals probably do not do as much writing as research, but writing still is a good part of the workload. The organization in each office is different, but paralegals may be called upon to analyze and summarize documents in discovery, to digest depositions, to write factual memoranda, and to do some preliminary drafting of documents or briefs. Good command of the rules of written English and a clear writing style will see you through. Again, this is not work you will do on your first day. A senior paralegal or the attorney charged with your orientation and training will instruct you as to what is expected of you with each writing task. Refer back to the R.O.S.C.O. writing productivity model discussed in Chapter 5 for more help.

Reading

A final dimension to the paperwork handled by a paralegal is the editing and proofreading. It goes without saying that the paralegal must edit and proofread his or her own work. He or she may also be called upon to edit attorneys' work and to proofread the work of the secretarial staff. Much of the editing and proofreading are done in the office. Occasionally, a paralegal may be sent directly to the printers to check out minutes of an important executive board meeting or a prospectus or other offering hot off the press. This type of assignment tends to be highly pressurized and to involve an all-nighter. The detail-minded paralegal who is willing to tackle such an assignment is well compensated for the extra effort.

The chief requirement of proofreading is attention to detail. The proofreader must give special attention first of all to the general sense of the material. Gaps in meaning generally occur when a line of text was inadvertently skipped in transcribing. If the material doesn't make logical sense, if it doesn't "hang together," read it again going back to the draft as needed. Everything that the writer intended must appear in the final copy. Beyond the overall meaning, proofreading and editing must give consideration to grammar and proper English usage. Agreement of tense and number are important, as are parallel constructions and use of the best word to convey the precise meaning.

The remainder of the proofreading task is more mechanical. It includes checking for misspellings; word repetition; word omission; transpositions of words, letters, or numbers; and accuracy of names, addresses, and all numbers.

Proofreading directly from the computer screen allows for instant correction of errors, but some paralegals find that they spare themselves eyestrain by proofreading the printed copy and then returning to make the corrections on the computer.

Here are some considerations for you to consider as you proofread:

- Scan the text for correctness of style and format, and for eye-appeal.

- Double-check the spelling of names; verify initials and addresses; ascertain accuracy of numbers.

- Check the continuity of numbered pages and of the numbered and lettered paragraphs or lists.

- Pay attention to prepositions that can vastly alter meaning.

- Do not rely solely on a computer spell checker. The spell checker can only spot gross errors; it does not distinguish between "pair," "pare," and "pear"; it does not know whether you meant to use the past tense or a plural.

If another person is available, it is often worthwhile to proofread together, especially if the letter or document is an important or technical one. If you proofread with a partner, hand the typewritten or printed page to him or her and read aloud from the original. Spell out names, addresses, and unusual words and pronounce endings very distinctly. Read numbers slowly.

When you proofread for your own benefit, you can mark up the page in any manner that is comprehensible to you. When you proofread for others in the office, you must follow some universal conventions but you can append clarifying notes and expand in plain English. Furthermore, you are available for consultation with your fellow workers in the office. However, when you edit or proofread material that is to be sent to typesetters or material that has come from the typesetter and is to be returned for correction, you must carefully follow rules for marking up proof. Following proofreaders' stylesheets is important when you are working on the printer's premises as well. Under time pressure it is most efficient to follow conventions.

The proofreaders' marks on page 151 come from the Government Printing Office *Manual of Style*. For the most part, these are universal markings. If your printer suggests some variations, take note and follow those where applicable.

If you are marking up a typescript with only one wide margin, you must use that one margin for all your proofreading marks. However, if you are marking printed material with ample margins on both sides, the system of marking proofs can be made easier by the use of an imaginary vertical line through the center of the type area. The placement of corrections in the left-hand margin for those errors found in the left-hand portion of the proof and in the right-hand margin for right-side errors prevents overcrowding of marks and facilitates corrections.

⊙ Insert period

↑ Insert comma

:/ Insert colon

;/ Insert semicolon

?/ Insert question mark

! Insert exclamation mark

=/ Insert hyphen

↲ Insert apostrophe

↲ ↲ Insert quotation marks

⇥ Insert 1-en dash

⇥ Insert 1-em dash

Insert space

⟍ᴅ> Insert ( ) points of space

shill Insert shilling (virgule or slash)

∨ Superior

∧ Inferior

(/) Parentheses

[/] Brackets

⬜ Indent 1 em

⬜⬜ Indent 2 ems

¶ Paragraph

no ¶ No paragraph

tr Transpose—used in margin

∼ Transpose—used in text

sp Spell out

ital Italic—used in margin

— Italic—used in text

b. f. Boldface—used in margin

∼∼∼ Boldface—used in text

s.c. Small caps—used in margin

≡ Small caps—used in text

rom. Roman type

caps. Caps—used in margin

≡ Caps—used in text

c+sc Caps & small caps—used in margin

≡ Caps & small caps—used in text

l.c. Lowercase—used in margin

/ Used in text to show deletion or substitution

ϟ Delete

⸙ Delete and close up

w. f. Wrong font (wrong size or style of type)

◡ Close up

⊐ Move right

⊏ Move left

⊓ Move up

⊔ Move down

‖ Align vertically

= Align horizontally

⊐⊏ Center horizontally

⊔⊓ Center vertically

eq. # Equalize space—used in margin

√/√ Equalize space—used in text

...... Let it stand—used in text

stet. Let it stand—used in margin

⊗ Letter(s) not clear

run over Carry over to next line

run back Carry back to preceding line

out, see copy Something omitted—see copy

ϟ/? Question to author to delete

(?) General query to author

∧ Caret—General indicator used to mark position of error

151

eight

REAPING THE REWARDS

"I'm a great believer in luck, and I find the harder I work the more I have of it."—Thomas Jefferson

And so we have come full circle in defining your role as a paralegal. Paralegals handle paperwork, organize the office, maintain and update client files, monitor the calendar, and research, write, and read. They serve as a liaison with clients, witnesses, other case participants, and outside professionals by gathering and imparting information. They meet, inform, interview, and prod to action. In addition paralegals seek out people, documents, and information, and compile and digest the information they gather. They write reports, negotiate with various parties, reassure and even do some measure of "hand-holding." They follow through on factual research and investigation, locating people, documents, and hard evidence as required.

Paralegals with good number skills find themselves doing asset inventories, income projections, and various other detailed tasks connected with the administration of wills, trusts, and estates. They may find themselves intimately involved with the financial aspects of matrimonial and child-custody cases.

Paralegals with excellent computer skills may find themselves producing spreadsheets and documents of various sorts. They may design forms which serve to expedite the work of the office and which make organization of information much more efficient. These computer-literate paralegals will find themselves at an advantage in using computer-assisted legal research programs and in producing the results of their research.

Paralegals with a strong research and investigational background will find challenge in tracking down hard-to-find information. They will develop a knack for finding the right people to ask the right questions about where to locate certain documents; about how, where, and when to file important court-related papers; about how to find missing witnesses, defendants, and clients using existing private help or public information sources from within the state, local, and federal governments.

Modern, competent paralegals are not afraid to do legwork outside the office or to get their hands covered with ink as they exploit information centers like police stations, libraries, and government offices. They will do whatever must be done to serve the client and the firm.

In exchange for the professional discretion and independence which paralegals are now given comes a demand for more training and greater job skills than ever before. The need for better-educated paralegals has given rise to the paralegal training industry. Attorneys take graduates of paralegal training programs and further indoctrinate them in methods, procedures, and requirements of the specific practice. There are also many continuing education courses in which paralegals can gather extra credits and add to their existing job skills and overall marketability.

As you gain in experience, you will be expected to do more work in less time, to handle more clients, to keep track of more files, to assist with court preparation and appearances, and generally to cover more cases. Attorneys will expect you to know more, to do more, and to think more for yourself. You will use more initiative, work more on your own, and supervise others as well.

Clearly, a paralegal is a professional, but a professional caught in a paradox. The paralegal has the independence of function and the responsibility of a professional but the status of a production worker. This paradox arises from the requirement that a paralegal always work under the supervision of an attorney. By this requirement attorneys are protected from intrusion upon their turf, from your unauthorized practice of law. From your standpoint, it means that you are protected from any ill results arising from your own errors. Since you work under the attorney's supervision, the attorney takes final responsibility for your actions. Of course your career can suffer from excess errors on your part, but you are never legally liable. This is clearly a benefit to you.

A further benefit of your status is financial. Paralegals are clearly the most professional of all workers who are classified in the "non-exempt" category. A worker who is classified as an exempt professional is paid a salary and is expected to work whatever hours are necessary to achieve a result. The professional often works far in excess of a normal forty-hour work week in order to fulfill professional responsibilities. The non-exempt worker, on the other hand, must, by law, be paid at overtime rates for work beyond the standard work week. Since paralegals are often called upon to put in many overtime hours—weekends, all-night stands, and just plain extra hours—the job becomes very lucrative. In short, paralegals may earn a lot of money.

The financial reward more than makes up for the lack of status and for the occasional snobbish disdain you may encounter. The further payoff comes with the tremendous self-satisfaction you feel when a matter settles and you know you played a major part.

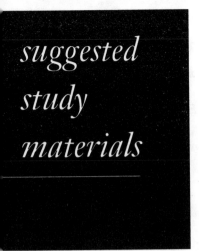

suggested study materials

Albrecht, Steve, *How to Write a Dynamite Business Letter!*, San Diego, CA: Shamrock Press, 1991.

Albrecht, Steve, *Painless Business Writing* (cassette tape), San Diego, CA: Shamrock Press, 1991.

Fins, Alice, *Opportunities in Paralegal Careers*, Lincolnwood, IL: VGM Career Horizons, 1985.

Golec, *Techniques of Legal Investigation*, Springfield, IL: Charles C. Thomas, 1985.

Grazian, Frank et al., *Glossary of Misused Words & Phrases*, Pitman, NJ: Communications Publications, 1989.

Lakein, Alan, *How to Get Control of Your Time and Your Life*, New York: Signet Books, 1973.

Larbalestrier, Deborah E., *Paralegal Practice and Procedure*, New York: Prentice-Hall, 1986.

Molick, Ellen K. et al., *The Legal Secretary's Resource*, Riverside, CA: Legal Secretaries, Inc., 1987.

Nemeth, Charles P., *The Paralegal Resource Manual*, Cincinnati: Anderson Publishing, 1989.

Shertzer, Margaret, *The Elements of Grammar*, New York: Macmillan, 1986.

Strunk, William Jr. & White, E.B., *The Elements of Style*, New York: Macmillan, 1979.

Wydick, Richard C., *Plain English for Lawyers*, Durham, NC: Carolina Academic Press, 1979.

paralegal organizations

American Bar Association Standing Committee on Legal Assistants
1155 East 60th St.
Chicago, IL 60637
(312) 988-50000

National Paralegal Association
P.O. Box 406
Solebury, PA 18963
(215) 297-8333

National Association of Legal Assistants
1601 South Main St., Suite 300
Tulsa, OK 74119
(918) 587-6828

National Center of Paralegal Training
3414 Peachtree Rd. NE, Suite 528
Atlanta, GA 30326
(404) 266-1060

National Federation of Paralegal Associations
P.O. Box 14103 (BFS)
Washington, DC 20044
(202) 659-0243

National Institute of Paralegal Training
1880 Howard Ave.
Vienna, VA 22183
(703) 442-0723

paralegal training programs

*T*his list of paralegal training programs was compiled by the American Bar Association. As of the publication of this book, those programs that have gained the accreditation of the Standing Committee on Legal Assistants of the American Bar Association are indicated by * (ABA Final Approval). Those with final approval still pending are indicated by ** (ABA Provisional Approval).

Since there is no centralized certification procedure for paralegals, there is no requirement that paralegals graduate from ABA-approved programs. The standards established for ABA approval are only guidelines for paralegal schools, not rigid rules. Seeking ABA approval is a voluntary activity which must be initiated by the school or program itself. Many very fine programs have consciously chosen to devote all their funds and energies to developing quality educational programs instead of satisfying the specific demands of certification inspection teams.

Approved and provisionally approved programs meet ABA standards, but do not discount more conveniently located or less expensive programs just because they lack this approval. Research each program that interests you. Ask about curricular offerings, on-site library and computer facilities, student-faculty ratio, the length of program, daily requirements, tuition costs, and their track record in placing graduates in paralegal positions.

ALABAMA

*Auburn University
Legal Assistant Education
Department of Justice &
Public Safety
Montgomery, AL 36193

Community College of the
Air Force
Maxwell Air Force Base
745 Selfridge, Maxwell, AFB
Montgomery, AL 36113

Draughons Junior College
Paralegal Program
5238 Millwood Road
Montgomery, AL 36109

Faulkner University,
Birmingham
2211 Magnolia Avenue
Birmingham, AL 35205

Faulkner University, Florence
1001 Florence Boulevard
Florence, AL 35630

Faulkner University, Mobile
1050 Government Street
Mobile, AL 36604

Faulkner University,
Montgomery
5345 Atlanta Highway
Montgomery, AL 36193

Huntington College
Continuing Education
1500 East Fairview Avenue
Montgomery, AL 36106

John C. Calhoun State
Community College
Paralegal Program
P.O. Box 2216
Decatur, AL 35602-2216

Miles College
Paralegal Studies
P.O. Box 3800
Birmingham, AL 35208

National Academy for
Paralegal Studies, Inc.
1572 Montgomery Hwy.,
Ste. 100
Birmingham, AL 35216

Northeast Alabama State
Junior College
P.O. Box 159
Rainsville, AL 35986

*Samford University
Division of Paralegal Studies
800 Lakeshore Drive
Birmingham, AL 35229

Southern Institute
Department of Paralegal
Studies
2015 Highland Avenue South
Birmingham, AL 35205

Spring Hill College
Legal Studies Program
Social Science Division
Mobile, AL 36608

University of Alabama,
Birmingham
UAB Special Studies
917 11th Street, South
Birmingham, AL 35294

University of Alabama
Paralegal Studies Program
917 Eleventh Street South
Birmingham, AL 35294

University of South
Alabama
Div. of C.E. & Evening
Studies
307 University Boulevard
Mobile, AL 36688

Wallace State Community
College
Highway 31, North
Hanceville, AL 35077

ALASKA

Alaska Business College
Paralegal Education
Department
800 East Dimond Boulevard
Suite 3-350
Anchorage, AK 99515

Charter College
4791 Business Park Boulevard
Number 6
Anchorage, AK 99503

University of Alaska,
Anchorage
Paralegal Certificate Program
School of Public Affairs,
Justice
3211 Providence Drive
Anchorage, AK 99508

University of Alaska, Juneau
Paralegal Studies Program
School of Business
Bill Ray Center
1108 F Street
Juneau, AK 99801

ARIZONA

Apollo College
Legal Assistant Program
13 West Westmore Road
Tucson, AZ 85705

Arizona State University
Paralegal Program
Center for Executive
   Development
College of Business
Tempe, AZ 85287-4306

Lamson College
1313 N. Second Street
Phoenix, AZ 84004

Lamson Junior College
Legal Assistant Program
1980 W. Main
Mesa, AZ 85201

Paralegal Institute (The)
1315 W. Indian
School Drawer 33903
Phoenix, AZ 85067

*Phoenix College
Legal Assistant Program
1202 W. Thomas Road
Phoenix, AZ 85013

*Pima Community College
Downtown Campus
1255 N. Stone Avenue
Tucson, AZ 85703

*Sterling School (The)
Legal Assistant Program
801 E. Indian School Road
Phoenix, AZ 85014

*The American Institute
Paralegal Studies Program
3443 N. Central, Suite 1800
Phoenix, AZ 85012

ARKANSAS

The Institute for Paralegal
   Training at
   South Central Career
   College
4500 W. Commercial Drive
North Little Rock, AR 72116

West Ark Community College
Legal Assistant Program
Grand Avenue
Ft. Smith, AR 72913

West Arkansas Community
  College
Division of Business
P.O. Box 3649
Ft. Smith, AR 72913

CALIFORNIA

American Paralegal Institute
21704 Golden Triangle
  Road
Suite 314
Santa Clarita, CA 91350

American River College
4700 College Oak Drive
Sacramento, CA 95841

Associated Business Programs
Paralegal Program
3763 Arlington Avenue,
  Ste. 2
Riverside, CA 92506

Barclay Career Schools
3460 Wilshire Boulevard
Suite 1111
Los Angeles, CA 90010

Barclay College
Legal Assistant Program
5172 Orange Avenue
Cypress, CA 90630

CSB Plus
Attorney Assistant Certificate
  Program
Extended Studies and
  Regional Programs
9001 Stockdale Highway
Bakersfield, CA 93311-1099

*California State University,
  Los Angeles
Certificate Program for the
  Legal Assistant
5151 State University Drive
Los Angeles, CA 90032

California College of Paralegal
  Studies
5121 Van Nuys Boulevard
Sherman Oaks, CA 91403

California State University,
  Chico
Department of Political
  Science
Paralegal Certificate Program
Chico, CA 95929-0455

California State University,
  Dominiguez Hills
Public Paralegal Cert.
  Program
School of Social and
  Behavorial Sciences
Carson, CA 90747

California State University,
San Bernardino
Paralegal Program
Political Science Dept.
5500 University Parkway
San Bernardino, CA 92407

California State University,
Hayward
Paralegal Certificate Program
Div. of Extended Educ.
Hayward, CA 94542

Cañada College
4200 Farm Hill Boulevard
Redwood City, CA 94061

Career Community College of
Business
Paralegal Program
7219 Escalante Way
Citrus Heights, CA 95610

*Cerritos College
11110 East Alondra
Boulevard
Norwalk, CA 90650

City College of San
Francisco
A.A. & Cert. Legal
Assistant Programs
50 Phelan Avenue
San Francisco, CA 94112

*Coastline Community College
11460 Warner Avenue
Fountain Valley, CA 92708

*College of The Sequoias
Paralegal Program
915 South Mooney Boulevard
Visalia, CA 93227

College of the Redwoods
Business Division
7351 Tompkins Hill Road
Eureka, CA 95501-9302

De Anza College
Legal Assistant Program
21250 Stevens Creek
Boulevard
Cupertino, CA 95014

Dominican College of San
Rafael
San Rafael, CA 94901

*El Camino College
Legal Assistant Program
16007 Crenshaw Boulevard
Torrance, CA 90506

Ewing University
Paralegal Program
2007 East Compton Blvd.
Compton, CA 90221

Fresno City College
1101 E. University Avenue
Fresno, CA 93741

Fullerton College
Legal Assistant Program
406 N. Adams Avenue
Fullerton, CA 92632

Humphreys College
6650 Inglewood Drive
Stockton, CA 92507

Imperial Valley College
P.O. Box 158
Imperial, CA 92251

Lake Tahoe Community
  College
Legal Assistant Certificate
2659 Lake Tahoe Blvd.
P.O. Box 14445
So. Lake Tahoe, CA 95702

Los Angeles City College
Law Department
855 North Vermont Avenue
Los Angeles, CA 90029

Los Angeles Mission College
Paralegal Program
1212 San Fernando Road
San Fernando, CA 91340

Los Angeles Southwest
  College
Legal Assistant Program
1600 W. Imperial Highway
Los Angeles, CA 90047

MTI Western Business
  College
Legal Assistant Program
2731 Capital Avenue
Sacramento, CA 95816

Merritt College
12500 Campus Drive
Oakland, CA 94619

Metropolitan Business College
2390 Pacific College
Long Beach, CA 90806

Metropolitan Technical
  Institute & Business College
Legal Technician Program
1963 No. E. Street, Ste. A
San Bernardino, CA 92405

Muir Technical Programs
Paralegal Program
4304 Twain Avenue
San Diego, CA 92120

National Academy for
  Paralegal Studies, Inc.
8615 Knott Avenue, Suite 11
Buena Park, CA 90620

167

Orange Coast College
2701 Fairview Road
Costa Mesa, CA 92626

Pacific Coast College
118 W. Fifth Street
Santa Ana, CA 92701

Pacific College of Legal
   Careers
Paralegal Studies Program
580 University Avenue
Sacramento, CA 95825

Pacific Legal Arts College
1387 Del Norte Road
Camarillo, CA 93010

Pasadena City College
Business Department
1570 E. Colorado Boulevard
Pasadena, CA 91106

Phillips College
Inland Empire Campus
4300 Central Avenue
Riverside, CA 92506

*Rancho Santiago College
Seventeenth at Bristol
Santa Ana, CA 92706

*Rio Hondo Community
   College
Paralegal Program
3600 Workman Mill Road
Whittier, CA 90608

Rutledge College
5620 Kearney Mesa Road
San Diego, CA 92111

*Saddleback College
Legal Assisting Program
28000 Marguerite Parkway
Mission Viejo, CA 92692

*Saint Mary's College
Paralegal Program
P.O. Box 3052
Moraga, CA 94575

San Bernardino Valley College
Legal Administration Program
701 South Mt. Vernon Ave.
San Bernardino, CA 92403

San Francisco State
   University
Exten. Educ.–Paralegal
   Studies
1600 Holloway Avenue
San Francisco, CA 94132

San Joaquin College of Law
Paralegal Program
3385 E. Shields
Fresno, CA 93726

San Jose State University
Legal Assistant Studies/
   Continuing Education
One Washington Square
San Jose, CA 95192

Santa Clara University
Institute for Paralegal
Education
Lawhouse
Santa Clara, CA 95050

Sawyer College of Business
6832 Van Nuys Boulevard
Van Nuys, CA 91405

Skyline College
Paralegal Program
3300 College Drive
San Bruno, CA 94066

Sonoma State University
Attorney Assistant Program
Office of Extended Education
1801 E. Cotati Avenue
Rohnert Park, CA 94928

Southern California College of
Business & Law
595 W. Lambert
Brea, CA 92621

*UCLA Extension
Attorney Assistant Training
Program
10995 LeConte Avenue,
Ste. 517
Los Angeles, CA 90024

Unilex College
Paralegal Division
995 Market Street
San Francisco, CA 94103

*Univ. of California, Davis
University Extension
Legal Assisting Cert.
Program
Davis, CA 95616

Univ. of California, Extension
Certificate in Legal
Assistantship
Riverside, CA 92521

*Univ. of California,
Extension Program in Legal
Assistantship
P.O. Box AZ
Irvine, CA 92716

Univ. of California, Extension
Certificate Program in Legal
Assistantship
UCSB Extension
Santa Barbara, CA 93106

Univ. of California, Extension
Program in Legal
Assistantship
740 Front Street, Suite 155
Santa Cruz, CA 95060

*Univ. of California,
San Diego
Legal Assistant Training
Program
X-001
La Jolla, CA 92093

Univ. of Northern California
Paralegal School
816 H Street, Suite 108
Sacramento, CA 95814

Univ. of Southern California
Paralegal Program
Law Center–University Park
Los Angeles, CA 90089-0071

University of LaVerne
College of Law
1950 Third Street
LaVerne, CA 91750

*University of San Diego
Lawyer's Assistant Program
Room 318, Serra Hall
Alcala Park
San Diego, CA 92110

*University of West Los
  Angeles
School of Paralegal Studies
12201 Washington Place
Los Angeles, CA 90066

Watterson College
336 Rancheros Drive
Suite C
San Marcos, CA 92069

West Valley College
Office of Community
  Development
14000 Fruitvale Avenue
Saratoga, CA 95070

COLORADO

*Arapahoe Community College
Legal Assistant Program
5900 S. Santa Fe Drive
Littleton, CO 80120

Community College of Aurora
Legal Assistant Program
701 Chambers Road
Aurora, CO 80011

Community College of
  Denver
Auraria Campus Div.,
Room CA-313
1111 West Colfax
Denver, CO 80204

*Denver Paralegal Institute
Gen'l Prac. Legal Asst. Prog.
1401 19th Street
Denver, CO 80202

Metropolitan State College
Legal Assistant Program
1006 11th Street
Denver, CO 80204

National Academy for
  Paralegal Studies, Inc.
950 S. Cherry St.,
  Suite 1000
Denver, CO 80222

Parks Junior College
Paralegal Studies Department
9065 Grant Street
Denver, CO 80229

Pikes Peak Community College
5675 S. Academy Blvd.,
  Box 19
Colorado Springs, CO 80906

University of Denver
College of Law
Program of Adv. Prof.
  Development
200 W. 14th Avenue
Denver, CO 80204

University of Southern
  Colorado
School of Liberal Arts
2200 Bonforte Boulevard
Pueblo, CO 81001

CONNECTICUT

Branford Hall School of
  Business
Paralegal Diploma Program
9 Business Park Drive
Branford, CT 06405

Briarwood College
Legal Assistant/Paralegal
  Program
2279 Mount Vernon Road
Southington, CT 06489

Connecticut Institute for
Paralegal Studies, Inc.
441 Summer Street
Stamford, CT 06901

Fairfield University
North Benson Road
CNS-9
Fairfield, CT 06430

*Hartford College for
  Women
Legal Assistant Program
50 Elizabeth Street
The Counseling Center
Hartford, CT 06105

*Manchester Community
  College
Legal Assistant Program
60 Bidwell Street
Manchester, CT 06040

*Mattatuck Community
  College
Legal Assistant Program
750 Chase Parkway
Waterbury, CT 06708

National Academy for
Paralegal Studies, Inc.
339 Main Street
P. O. Box 4102
Yalesville, CT 06492

*Norwalk Community College
Legal Assistant Program
333 Wilson Avenue
Norwalk, CT 06854

Post College
Legal Assistant Program
800 Country Club Road
Waterbury, CT 06708

*Quinnipiac College
Legal Studies Department
Mount Carmel Avenue
Hamden, CT 06518

*Sacred Heart University
5151 Park Avenue
Fairfield, CT 06432

*University of Bridgeport
Law Center/Legal Assistant
  Program
303 University Avenue
Bridgeport, CT 06601

University of New Haven
Paralegal Studies
300 Orange Avenue
West Haven, CT 06516

DELAWARE

Brandywine College of
Widener University
P.O. Box 7139, Concord Pike
Wilmington, DE 19803

Delaware Tech. & Cmty.
  College
Southern Campus
Legal Assistant Technology
Georgetown, DE 19947

National Academy for
  Paralegal Studies, Inc.
300 Delaware Ave., 10th Fl.
P.O. Box 1960
Wilmington, DE 19801

University of Delaware
Legal Assistant Education
  Program
2800 Pennsylvania Avenue
Wilmington, DE 19806

*Wesley College
Paralegal Studies Program
Dover, DE 19901

*Widener University
Inst. for Prof. Development
706 Market Street Mall
Law and Education Center
Wilmington, DE 19801

DISTRICT OF COLUMBIA

Antioch School of Law
Paralegal Program
1624 Crescent Place N.W.
Washington, DC 20009

*George Washington
University
Ctr. for Career Educ. &
Workshops
801 22nd Street, N.W.
Suite T409
Washington, DC 20052

*Georgetown University
Legal Assistant Program
School for Summer & Contin-
uing Education
Washington, DC 20057

Institute of Law and Aging
Paralegal Training Program
National Law Center,
Ste. T401
George Washington Univ.
801 22nd Street, N.W.
Washington, DC 20052

University of the District of
Columbia
1331 H Street, N.W.
Washington, DC 20005

FLORIDA

American Institute for
Paralegal Studies, Inc.
Southeast Regional Office
5700 St. Augustine Road
Jacksonville, FL 32207

Barry University
Legal Assistant Institute
11300 N.E. Second Avenue
Miami Shores, FL 33161

Barry University
Legal Assistant Institute
Ft. Lauderdale, FL 33310

Barry University
Legal Assistant Institute
Naples, FL 33941

*Broward Community College
Legal Assistant Program
7200 Hollywood/Pines
Boulevard
Pembroke Pines, FL 33024

Career Training Institute
Paralegal Studies Program
2120 West Colonial Drive
Orlando, FL 32804

Central Florida
Community College
P.O. Box 1388
Ocala, FL 32670

Charron Williams College
Legal Assistant Program
6289 West Sunrise Blvd.
Ft. Lauderdale, FL 33313

Edison Community College
P.O. Box 06210
Ft. Myers, FL 33906-6210

Florida Atlantic University
Institute for Legal Assistants
Div. of Continuing Education
Boca Raton, FL 33431

Fort Lauderdale College
Legal Assistant Studies
  Program
100 E. Broward Blvd.
Fort Lauderdale, FL 33301

Hillsborough Community
  College
P.O. Box 30030
Tampa, FL 33620

Jones College
Paralegal Degree & Diploma
  Programs
Miami Campus
255 S.W. 8th Street
Miami, FL 33130

Jones College
Ft. Lauderdale Campus
6289 W. Sunrise Boulevard
Ft. Lauderdale, FL 33313

Jones College, Lakeland
  Campus
Paralegal Degree & Diploma
  Programs
2620 Kathleen Road
Lakeland, FL 33809

Jones College, South Campus
Paralegal Degree & Diploma
  Programs
3428 Beach Boulevard
Jacksonville, FL 32207

Legal Career Institute
Paralegal Program
5225 West Broward Blvd.
Plantation, FL 33317

Legal Career Institute
Paralegal Program
7289 Garden Road
Riviera Beach, FL 33404

Manatee Junior College
Legal Assistant Program
P.O. Box 1849
Bradenton, FL 33507

*Miami-Dade Community
  College
Legal Assistant Program
Mitchell Wolfson New World
  Center
300 N.E. 2nd Avenue
Miami, FL 33132

National Center for Paralegal
  Training
Lawyer's Assistant Program
1460 Brickell Avenue,
  Ste. 200
Miami, FL 33131

National Center for Paralegal
  Training
Lawyer's Assistant Program
1799 S.E. 17th Street
Ft. Lauderdale, FL 33316

Orlando College
Paralegal Program
925 South Orange Avenue
Orlando, FL 32806

PRS Career Academy, Inc.
Legal Studies Program
2648 West Highway 434
Longwood, FL 32779

Palm Beach Jr. College
4200 Congress Avenue
Lake Worth, FL 33461

Palm Beach Jr. College,
  North
3160 PGA Boulevard
Palm Beach Gdns., FL 33410

Paralegal Careers, Inc.
1211 N. Westshore
Suite 100
Tampa, FL 33607

Pensacola Jr. College
Legal Assistant Program
1000 College Boulevard
Pensacola, FL 32504

*Santa Fe Community
  College
Legal Assistant Program
3000 N.W. 83rd Street
Gainesville, FL 32601-1530

Sarasota Voc/Tech.
  Center
Legal Assitant Program
4748 Beneva Road
Sarasota, FL 34231

South College
Paralegal Program
1760 North Congress Avenue
West Palm Beach, FL 33409

Southern Career Institute
164 W. Royal Palm Road
P.O. Box 2158
Boca Raton, FL 33432

*Southern College
Legal Assistant Program
5600 Lake Underhill Road
Orlando, FL 32807

St. Petersburg Junior College
Legal Assistant Program
Clearwater Campus
2465 Drew Street
Clearwater, FL 34625

Tampa College
Paralegal Program
3924 Coconut Palm Drive
Tampa, FL 33619

Tampa College of Lakeland
Paralegal Program
1200 U.S. Hwy. 98 South
Lakeland, FL 33801

University of Central Florida
Legal Studies Program
Department of Criminal
  Justice
Orlando, FL 32816-0395

University of Miami
Institute for Paralegal
  Studies
P.O. Box 248005
Coral Gables, FL 33124

University of North Florida
Paralegal Studies Institute
P.O. Box 17074,
  Pottsburg Sta.
Jacksonville, FL 32245-7074

University of West Florida
Legal Administration Program
Dept. of Political Science
11000 University Parkway
Pensacola, FL 32514

Valencia Community College
East Campus
P.O. Box 3028
Orlando, FL 32802

GEORGIA

Academy for Paralegal
  Studies
8493 Campbellton Street
Douglasville, GA 30133

American Institute for
  Paralegal Studies, Inc.
First Atlanta Tower
Suite 2400
Atlanta, GA 30383

**Athens Area Technical
  Institute
Paralegal Studies Program
U.S. Highway 29 North
Athens, GA 30610

Atlanta Paralegal Institute
1393 Peachtree Street, N.E.
Atlanta, GA 30309

Gainesville College
Legal Assistant Program
Mundy Mill Road
Gainesville, GA 30501

Morris Brown College
Legal Assistant Program
643 Martin Luther King Jr.
 Drive
Atlanta, GA 30314

*National Ctr. for Paralegal
 Training
Lawyer's Assistant Program
3414 Peachtree Road, N.E.
Suite 528
Atlanta, GA 30326

HAWAII

*Kapiolani Community College
Legal Assistant Program
620 Pensacola Avenue
Honolulu, HI 96814

IDAHO

National Academy for
 Paralegal Studies, Inc.
P.O. Box 4883
Pocatello, ID 83205

University of Idaho
College of Law
Paralegal Program
Moscow, ID 83840

ILLINOIS

American Institute for
 Paralegal Studies, Inc.
One South 450 Summit
 Avenue
Suite 230
Oakbrook Terrace, IL 60181

Elgin Community College
Legal Technology Program
1700 Spartan Drive
Elgin, IL 60123

Illinois Central
Paralegal Program
One College Drive
East Peoria, IL 61635

Illinois State University
Legal Studies Program
Schroeder 306
Political Science Dept.
Normal, IL 61761

*Loyola University
Institute for Paralegal
 Studies
Mallinckrodt Campus
1041 Ridge Road
Wilmette, IL 60091

MacCormac Junior College
615 North West Avenue
Elmhurst, Il 60126-1861

177

MacCormac Junior College
327 South LaSalle Street
Chicago, IL 60604

Midstate College
Paralegal Services
244 S.W. Jefferson, Box 148
Peoria, IL 61602

*Roosevelt University
Lawyer's Assistant Program
430 So. Michigan Avenue
Chicago, IL 60605

*Sangamon State University
Legal Studies Program
LSP PAC 429
Springfield, Il 62794-9243

*South Suburban College
Paralegal/Legal Asst. Program
15800 S. State Street
South Holland, IL 60473

*Southern Illinois University
at Carbondale
Paralegal Studies Program
Carbondale, IL 62901

Uptown Learning Center
Legal Assistant Training
Program
1220 West Wilson
Chicago, IL 60640

*William Rainey Harper College
Legal Technology Program
1200 W. Algonquin Road
Palatine, IL 60067-7398

INDIANA

American Institute for
Paralegal Studies, Inc.
52582 U.S. 31 N.
South Bend, IN 46637

*Ball State University
Legal Assistance & Legal
Administration
Muncie, IN 47306

CareerCom. Jr. College
of Business
1314 Burch Drive
Evansville, IN 47711

Indiana Central University
1400 E. Hanna Avenue
Indianapolis, IN 46227

Indiana State University
Conferences & Non-Credit
Programs
Alumni Center, Room 240
Terre Haute, IN 47809

Indiana University at South
Bend
Paralegal Studies Certificate
1700 Meshawaka Avenue
South Bend, IN 46634

Lockyear College
Legal Assistant Program
1200 Waterway Boulevard
Indianapolis, IN 46202

*University of Evansville
Legal Paraprofessional
   Program
1800 Lincoln Avenue
Evansville, IN 47722

*Vincennes University
Paralegal Program
1002 North 1st Street
Vincennes, IN 47591

IOWA

*Des Moines Area
   Community College
Legal Assistant Program
   Urban Campus
1100 7th Street
Des Moines, IA 50314

Iowa Lakes Community
   College
Legal Assistant Program
300 South 18th Street
Estherville, IA 51334

*Kirkwood Community College
6301 Kirkwood Boulevard, S.W.
P.O. Box 2068
Cedar Rapids, IA 52406

Marycrest College
1607 West 12th Street
Davenport, IA 52804

National Academy for
   Paralegal Studies, Inc.
627 Frances Building
Sioux City, IA 51101

KANSAS

Barton County Community
   College
Legal Assisting
Great Bend, KS 67530

Hutchinson Community
   College
Legal Assistant Program
1300 North Plum
Hutchinson, KS 67501

*Johnson County Community
   College
Paralegal Program
12345 College at Quivera
Overland Park, KS 66210

National Academy for
   Paralegal Studies, Inc.
105 South Kansas
Olathe, KS 66061

Southern Technical College
Legal Assisting Program
2015 South Meridan
Wichita, KS 67213

The Brown Mackie College
Legal Assistant Program
8000 W. 110th Street
Overland Park, KS 66210

Washburn University of
Topeka
Legal Assistant Program
17th & College
Topeka, KS 66621

*Wichita State University
Legal Assistant Program
College of Business Admin.
Wichita, KS 67208

KENTUCKY

*Eastern Kentucky University
Paralegal Programs
McCreary 113
Richmond, KY 40475-3122

*Institute for Paralegal
Studies at Sullivan College
3101 Bardstown Road
Louisville, KY 40205

Institute for Paralegal Studies
at Sullivan College
2659 Regency Road
Lexington, KY 40503

*Midway College
Paralegal Studies Program
Midway, KY 40347

Morehead State University
Paralegal Program
College of Arts and Sciences
Morehead, KY 40351

National Academy for
Paralegal Studies, Inc.
P.O. Box 1291
Frankfort, KY 40602

*University of Louisville
Paralegal Program
106 Ford Hall
Political Science Dept.
Louisville, KY 40292

LOUISIANA

Institute for Legal Studies
3501 N. Causeway Boulevard
Suite 900
Metairie, LA 70002

Louisiana State University
Paralegal Studies Program
361 Pleasant Hall–LSU
Baton Rouge, LA 70803

Louisiana State University in
  Shreveport
Paralegal Institute
Division of Continuing
  Education & Special
  Programs
Shreveport, LA 71115

Nicholls State University
Legal Assistant Studies
P.O. Box 2089
Thibodaux, LA 70310

Phillips Junior College
Paralegal Studies Program
5001 West Bank Expressway
Marrero, LA 70072

Phillips Junior College
Paralegal Studies Program
822 South Clearview Avenue
New Orleans, LA 70123

Southwest Paralegal College
115 East Main Street
Lafayette, LA 70501

*Tulane University
  University College
  Paralegal Studies Program
  6823 St. Charles Avenue
  New Orleans, LA 70118

University of New Orleans
Metropolitan College
Paralegal Institute
226 Carondelet, Ste. 310
New Orleans, LA 70130

Univ. of Southwestern Louisi-
  ana University College
P.O. Box 43370
Lafayette, LA 70504-3370

MAINE

Beal College
Paralegal Program
629 Main Street
Bangor, ME 04401

National Academy for
  Paralegal Studies, Inc.
P.O. Box 1028
Rockland, ME 04841

National Academy for
  Paralegal Studies, Inc.
Paralegal Studies, Inc.
RFD 3, Box 2470
Waterville, ME 04901

University of Maine
University College
Legal Technology Program
Katahdin Hall
210 Texas Avenue
Bangor, ME 04401

University of Southern Maine
Dept. of Community
  Programs
USM Intown Center
68 High Street
Portland, ME 04101

MARYLAND

Anne Arundel Community
College
Paralegal Studies Program
101 College Parkway
Careers Bldg., Room 234
Arnold, MD 21012

Community College of
Baltimore
Harbor Paralegal Program
Lombard Street at Market
Place
Baltimore, MD 21202

*Dundalk Community College
7200 Sollers Point Road
Baltimore, MD 21222

Harford Community College
Adult Occupational
Education
401 Thomas Run Road
Bel Air, MD 21014

Montgomery College
Legal Assistant Program
Takoma Park, MD 20912

National Academy for
Paralegal Studies, Inc.
P.O. Box 20148
Eudowood, MD 21284

Prince George's Community
College
Paralegal Program
301 Largo Road
Largo, MD 20772-2199

University of Maryland
University College
College Park Campus
College Park, MD 20742

*Villa Julie College
Paralegal Program
Green Spring Valley Road
Stevenson, MD 21153

MASSACHUSETTS

*Anna Maria College
Paralegal Program
Sunset Lane
Paxton, MA 01612-1198

Assumption College
Paralegal Studies
500 Salisbury Street
Center for Continuing & Pro-
fessional Education
Worcester, MA 01609

Bay Path College Legal
Assistant Program
588 Longmeadow Street
Longmeadow, MA 01106

Becker Junior College
Paralegal Studies Program
61 Sever Street
Worcester, MA 01609

*Bentley College
Institute of Paralegal Studies
Beaver & Forest Streets
Waltham, MA 02254

Boston State College
Paralegal Program
625 Huntington Avenue
Boston, MA 02115

Boston University
Metropolitan College
Legal Assistant Program
755 Commonwealth Avenue
Boston, MA 02215

*Elms College
Paralegal Institute
Chicopee, MA 01013

Hampshire College
Amherst, MA 01002
Kathryn Gibbs School
Legal Assistant Program
5 Arlington Street
Boston, MA 02116

Middlesex Community
  College
Paralegal Studies Program
Terrace Hall Avenue
Burlington, MA 01803

Mount Ida College
Paralegal Studies Program
777 Dedham Street
Newton Centre, MA 02159

National Academy for
  Paralegal Studies, Inc.
53 Winter Street
Weymouth, MA 02189

Newbury College
Paralegal Program
921 Boylston Street
Boston, MA 02115

North Shore Community
  College
3 Essex Street
Beverly, MA 02193

Northeastern University
Paralegal Program
Center for Continuing
  Education
370 Common Street
Dedham, MA 02026

*Northern Essex Community
  College
Paralegal Studies Program
Elliott Street
Haverhill, MA 01830

Regis College
Legal Studies Program
235 Wellesley Street
Weston, MA 02193

Suffolk University
College of Liberal Arts &
  Sciences
Lawyer's Assistant
  Certificate
Beacon Hill
Boston, MA 02114-4280

Univ. of Massachusetts–
  Boston
Center for Legal Education
  Services
Downtown Center
Boston, MA 02125

MICHIGAN

American Institute for
  Paralegal Studies, Inc.
Southfield Regional Office
Honewell Ctr., Ste. 225
17515 W. Nine Mile Road
Southfield, MI 48075

Davenport College
Paralegal Program
4123 West Main Street
Kalamazoo, MI 49007

*Eastern Michigan University
Legal Assistant (Paralegal)
  Program
Business and Industrial Educ.
College of Technology
Ypsilanti, MI 48197

*Ferris State University
Legal Assistant Program
Big Rapids, MI 49307

Grand Valley State College
School of Public Service
College Landing
467 Mackinac Hall
Allendale, MI 49401

Henry Ford Community
  College
22586 Ann Arbor Trail
Dearborn Heights, MI 48127

Henry Ford Community
  College
5101 Evergreen Road
Dearborn, MI 48128

*Kellogg Community College
Legal Assistant Program
450 North Avenue
Battle Creek, MI 49016

Lake Superior State College
A.S. & B.A. Legal Assistant
  Programs
Social Science Department
Sault Ste. Marie, MI 49783

*Lansing Community College
Legal Assistant Program
Criminal Justice & Law Center
419 N. Capitol Avenue
P.O. Box 40010
Lansing, MI 48901-7210

*Macomb Community College
South Campus
14500 Twelve Mile Road
Warren, MI 48093

*Madonna University
36600 Schoolcraft Road
Livonia, MI 48150

Michigan Christian College
800 West Avon Road
Rochester, MI 48063

Michigan Paralegal Institute
65 Cadillac Square
Suite 3200
Detroit, MI 48226

Mott Community Hospital
1401 E. Court Street
Flint, MI 48503

Oakland Community College
Orchard Ridge Campus
27055 Orchard Lake Road
Farmington Hills, MI 48018

*Oakland University
Diploma Pgm. for Legal
  Assistants
Div. of Continuing
  Education
Rochester, MI 48309-4401

St. Clair County Community
  College
323 Erie Street
Port Huron, MI 48060

*University of Detroit Mercy
Legal Asst./Legal Admn.
  Program
8200 W. Outer Drive
Detroit, MI 48219

MINNESOTA

*Hamline University
Legal Assistant Program
1536 Hewitt Avenue
St. Paul, MN 55104-1284

*Inver Hills Community
  College
Legal Assistant Program
8445 College Trail
Inver Grove Hgts., MN
  55076

*Minnesota Legal Assistant
  Institute
12450 Wayzata Boulevard
Minneapolis, MN 55343

Moorhead State University
Legal Assistant Program
11th Street South
Moorhead, MN 56560-9980

*North Hennepin
   Community College
Legal Assistant Program
7411 85th Avenue North
Minneapolis, MN 55445

*Winona State University
Paralegal Program
Minne Hall
Winona, MN 55987

MISSISSIPPI

Hinds Community College
Paralegal Technology Program
Raymond, MS 39154

*Mississippi University for
   Women
Paralegal Program
Div. of Business & Economics
College Street
Columbus, MS 39701

Northwest Mississippi Jr.
   College
Legal Assistant Program
300 North Panola Street
Senatobia, MS 38668

*Univ. of Southern Mississippi
Paralegal Studies Program
Hattiesburg & Gulf Pk
   Campuses
Hattiesburg, MS 39406-5101

University of Mississippi
Tupelo Campus
Paralegal Studies Program
655 Eason Boulevard
Tupelo, MS 38801

University of Mississippi
Paralegal Studies Program
Universities Center
   Campus
3825 Ridgewood Road
Jackson, MS 39211

MISSOURI

*Avila College
Legal Assistant Program
11901 Wornall Road
Kansas City, MO 64145

Concorde Career Institute
Legal Assistant Program
P.O. Box 26610
Kansas City, MO 64196

Drury Evening College
Continuing Education
   Division
Legal Assistant Studies
900 North Benton Avenue
Springfield, MO 65802

Marysville College
13550 Conway Road
St. Louis, MO 63110

Mid-American Paralegal
    Institute
8008 Carondelet, Suite 211
St. Louis, MO 63105

*Missouri Western State
    College
4525 Downs Drive
St. Joseph, MO 64507

National Academy for
    Paralegal Studies, Inc.
11907 Manchester Road
St. Louis, MO 63131

Penn Valley Community
    College
Legal Technology Program
3201 S.W. Trafficway
Kansas City, MO 64111

Platt Junior College
Legal Assistant Program
3131 Frederick Avenue
St. Joseph, MO 64506-2911

Rockhurst College
Paralegal Studies
1100 Rockhurst Road
Kansas City, MO 64110

Rutledge College
Legal Assistant Program
625 North Benton
Springfield, MO 65806

Southeast Missouri State
    University
900 Normal
Cape Girardeau, MO 63701

St. Louis Community College
    at Meramec
11333 Big Bend
St. Louis, Mo 63122

St. Louis Community College
    at Florissant Valley
3400 Perhall Road
St. Louis, MO 63135

*Webster University
Legal Studies Program
470 East Lockwood Avenue
St. Louis, MO 63119-3194

William Jewell College
Paralegal Program
Evening Division
Liberty, Mo 64068

*William Woods College
Paralegel Studies Program
Fulton, MO 65252

MONTANA

College of Great Falls
Paralegal Studies
1301 20th Street South
Great Falls, MT 59405

Missoula Voc. Tech. Center
Legal Assisting Cert. Program
909 South Avenue West
Missoula, MT 59801

Rocky Mountain College
Legal Assistant Program
1511 Poly Drive
Billings, MT 59102-1796

NEBRASKA

*College of St. Mary
Paralegal Studies Program
1901 South 72nd Street
Omaha, NE 68124

Lincoln School of Commerce
Legal Studies Program
1821 K Street
P.O. Box 82826
Lincoln, NE 68501

*Metropolitan Community
College
Legal Asst./Paralegal
Program
P.O. Box 3777
Omaha, NE 68103-0777

Nebraska College of
Business
Legal Assistant Program
3636 California Street
Omaha, NE 68131

Nebraska Wesleyan College
Legal Assistant Program
Lincoln, NE 68504

VTI Career Institute of
Omaha
Legal Assistant Program
32nd Avenue and Dodge
Streets
Omaha, NE 68131

NEVADA

Clark County Community
College
Legal Assistant Program
3200 East Cheyenne Avenue
North Las Vegas, NV 89030

Las Vegas Business College
Legal Assistant Program
2917 West Washington Avenue
Las Vegas, NV 89107

Reno Business College
Paralegal Program
140 Washington Street
Reno, NV 89503

NEW HAMPSHIRE

McIntosh College
Legal Assistant Program
23 Cataract Avenue
Dover, NH 03820

National Academy for
  Paralegal Studies, Inc.
97 West Merrimack Street
Manchester, NH 03101

Notre Dame College
Legal Assistant Program
2321 Elm Street
Manchester, NH 03104

*Rivier College
Baccalaureate and Certificate
  Paralegal Studies
Nashua, NH 03060

University of New
  Hampshire
Paralegal Studies Program
24 Rosemary Lane
Durham, NH 03824

NEW JERSEY

American Institute for
  Paralegal Studies, Inc.
75 South Brookline Drive
Laurel Springs, NJ 08021

Atlantic Community College
Paralegal Program
Mays Landing, NJ 08330

Bergen Community College
400 Paramus Road
Paramus, NJ 07652

Brookdale Community College
765 Newman Springs Road
Lincroft, NJ 07738

Burlington County College
CA 267
Pemberton-Brown Mills
  Road
Pemberton, NJ 08068

*Cumberland County College
Legal Technology Program
P.O. Box 517
Vineland, NJ 08360

*Fairleigh Dickinson University
Paralegal Studies Program
285 Madison Avenue
Madison, NJ 07940

First School for Careers
Paralegal Division
110 Main Avenue
Passaic Park, NJ 07055

Harris School of Business
Paralegal Studies Program
654 Longwood Avenue
Cherry Hill, NJ 08002

Institute of Paralegal Studies
453 North Wood Avenue
Linden, NJ 07036

Juris-Tech
The Paralegal School
100 West Prospect
Waldwick, NJ 07463

Law Center for Paralegal
   Studies
374 Millburn Avenue
Suite 200
Millburn, NJ 07041

*Mercer County Community
   College
Legal Assistant Program
P.O. Box B
Trenton, NJ 08690

*Middlesex County College
Legal Studies Department
155 Mill Road
P.O. Box 3050
Edison, NJ 08818-3050

*Montclair State College
Department of Legal Studies
Paralegal Studies Program
Upper Montclair, NJ 07043

National Academy for
   Paralegal Studies, Inc.
One Lethbridge Plaza,
   Suite 23
P.O. Box 835
Mahwah, NJ 07430

Ocean County College
Legal Assistant Technology
   Program
Toms River, NJ 08753

Plaza School
Garden State Plaza
Route 17 & Route 4
Paramus, NJ 07652

Raritan Valley Community
   College
Legal Assisting Program
P.O. Box 3300
Sommerville, NJ 08876

South Jersey Paralegal
   School
302 Sherry Way
Cherry Hill, NJ 08034

Taylor Business Institute
250 Route 28
Post Office Box 6875
Bridgewater, NJ 08807

Union Institute of Paralegal
  Studies
427 Chestnut Street
Union, NJ 07083

Upsala College
Paralegal Program
Beck Hall, 203
East Orange, NJ 07019

NEW MEXICO

Albuquerque Tech/Voc.
  Institute
Legal Assistant Program
4700 Morris, N.E.
Albuquerque, NM 87111

Navajo Community College
Legal Advocates Training
  Program
P.O. Box 580
Shiprock, NM 87420

Santa Fe Community
  College
Paralegal Studies Program
South Richards Avenue
P.O. Box 4187
Santa Fe, NM 87502

University of Albuquerque
St. Joseph's Place, N.W.
Albuquerque, NM 87105

NEW YORK

*Adelphi University
  Center for Career Programs
  Lawyer's Assistant Program
  Garden City, L.I., NY 11530

American Career Schools,
  Inc.
1707 Veterans Highway
Central Islip, NY 11722

American Career Schools,
  Inc.
130 Ontario Street
Albany, NY 12206

American News Institute
  Programs
110 Central Park Avenue
  South
Hartsdale, NY 10530

Baruch College
Paralegal Certificate Program
17 Lexington Avenue
Box 409
New York, NY 10010

*Bronx Community College
  University Ave. & W. 181 St.
  Bronx, NY 10453

Brooklyn College
Paralegal Program
1212 Boylan Hall
Brooklyn, NY 11210

Broome Community College
Paralegal Assistant Program
P.O. Box 1017
Binghamton, NY 13902

Corning Community College
Paralegal Assistant Program
Spencer Hill Road
Corning, NY 14830

*Elizabeth Seton College
Legal Assistant Program
1061 North Broadway
Yonkers, NY 10701

Erie Community College
Paralegal Unit
121 Ellicott Street
Buffalo, NY 14209

Herkimer County Community
 College
Paralegal Program
Herkimer, NY 13350

*Hilbert College
Legal Assistant Program
5200 South Park Avenue
Hamburg, NY 14075

International Career Institute
Paralegal Program
120 West 30th Street
New York, NY 10001

Iona College
Legal Assistant Program
715 North Avenue
New Rochelle, NY 10801

Junior College of Albany
140 New Scotland Avenue
Albany, NY 12208

Kingsborough Community
 College
City University of New York
Office of Continuing
 Education
Paralegal Studies Program
Brooklyn, NY 11235

*Lehman College of the
 City University of
 New York
Paralegal Studies Program
Office of Cont. Education
Bedford Park Blvd. West
Bronx, NY 10468

Long Island University
Rockland Campus
Route 340
Sparkill, NY 10976

*Long Island University
Brooklyn Center
Paralegal Studies Program
University Plz.-LLC 302
Brooklyn, NY 11201-5372

*Long Island University
C.W. Post Campus
Paralegal Studies Program
Greenvale, NY 11548

*Manhattanville College
Paralegal Program
Office of Special Programs
Purchase, NY 10577

*Marist College
Paralegal Program
North Road
Poughkeepsie, NY 12601-1381

Marymount Manhattan
College
Paralegal Studies Program
221 East 71st Street
New York, NY 10021

Mercy College
Paralegal Studies Program
Dept. of Law, Criminal
Justice
555 Broadway
Dobbs Ferry, NY 10522

*Mercy College
White Plains Extension
Center
Paralegal Studies Program
White Plains, NY 10601

*Nassau Community College
Paralegal Program
Stewart Avenue
Garden City, NY 11530-6793

National Academy for
Paralegal Studies, Inc.
P.O. Box 517
Suffern, NY 10901

*New York City Technical
College of the City
University of New York
300 Jay Street, Room N-422
Brooklyn, NY 11201-2983

New York Institute of
Technology
Paralegal Studies Program
Building 66–Room 131
Carlton Avenue
Central Islip, NY 11722

*New York University
Institute of Paralegal
Studies
11 West 42nd Street
New York, NY 10036

Niagara County Community
College
Legal Assistant Program
3111 Saunders Settlement Road
Sanborn, NY 14132

Paralegal Institute
132 Nassau Street
New York, NY 10038

*Queens College/CUNY
Continuing Education Program
Paralegal Studies
Flushing, NY 11367

Rockland Community College
Legal Assistant Program
145 College Road
Suffern, NY 10901

Schenectady County
   Community College
Paralegal Program
78 Washington Avenue
Schenectady, NY 12305

St. John's University
Legal Assistant Program
Grand Central & Utopia
   Pkwy.
Jamaica (Queens), NY 11439

*Suffolk County Community
   College
A.A.S. Legal Assistant
   Program
533 College Road
Selden, NY 11784

Sullivan County Community
   College
Paralegal Program
Loch Sheldrake, NY 12759

*Syracuse University College
Legal Assistant Program
610 East Fayette Street
Syracuse, NY 13244-6020

The City University of New
   York
St. George Campus
130 Stuyvesant Place
Staten Island, NY 10301

The New School
Paralegal Studies
66 West 12th Street
New York, NY 10011

The Sobelsohn School
Paralegal Program
352 Seventh Avenue
New York, NY 10001

NORTH CAROLINA

Appalachian State University
Department of Criminal
   Justice and Political
   Science
Boone, NC 28606

*Carteret Community College
Paralegal Technology Program
3505 Arendell Street
Morehead City, NC 28557

Cecils Jr. College of Business
1567 Patton Avenue
Asheville, NC 28806

Central Carolina Tech.
Institute
Department of Community
Colleges
1105 Kelly Drive
Sanford, NC 27330

Central Piedmont Community
College
Paralegal Technology Program
1201 Elizabeth Avenue
P.O. Box 35009
Charlotte, NC 28235

Coastal Carolina Community
College
Paralegal Technology Program
444 Western Blvd.
Jacksonville, NC 28540

Davidson County Community
College
Intersection of Old
Greensboro Road &
Interstate 40
Lexington, NC 27292

*Fayetteville Tech. Community
College
Paralegal Technology Program
P.O. Box 5236
Fayetteville, NC 28303

Greensboro College
Applied Arts & Social
Sciences
815 West Market Street
Greensboro, NC 27401-1875

Johnston Community
College
Paralegal Program
P.O. Box 2350
Smithfield, NC 27577-2350

*Meredith College
Legal Assistant Program
3800 Hillsborough Street
Raleigh, NC 27607-5298

Pitt Technical Institute
Paralegal Program
P.O. Drawer 7007
Greenville, NC 27834

Southwestern Technical
Institute
P.O. Box 95
Sylva, NC 28779

NORTH DAKOTA

National Academy for
Paralegal Studies, Inc.
116 North Fourth Street
Bismarck, ND 58502

University of North Dakota
Lake Region
Legal Assistant Program
Devils Lake, ND 58301

OHIO

American Institute for
  Paralegal Studies, Inc.
2999 E. Dublin-Granville Rd.
Suite 217
Columbus, OH 43229

American Retraining Center
Paralegal Program
1900 Euclid Avenue,
  Ste. 801
Cleveland, OH 44115

*Capital University Law
  Center
Legal Assistant Program
665 South High Street
Columbus, OH 43215

Clark Technical College
Box 570
Springfield, OH 45501

College of Mount St. Joseph
Legal Assistant Program
Suburban Cincinnati
Mount St. Joseph, OH 45051

*Dyke College
Paralegal Education Programs
112 Prospect Avenue
Cleveland, OH 44115

Hammel College
885 E. Buchtel
Akron, OH 44305

Muskingum Area Technical
  College
Paralegal Program
1555 Newark Road
Zanesville, OH 43701

National Academy for
  Paralegal Studies, Inc.
9319 Cincinnati-Columbus
  Road
West Chester, OH 45069

Ohio Paralegal Academy
209 South High Street
Suite 507
Columbus, OH 43215

Paralegal Institute of the West-
  ern Reserve Academy
Silver Building, Suite 201
Public Square
Wooster, OH 44691

*Sinclair Community College
Legal Assisting Program
444 West Third Street
Dayton, OH 45402

*University of Cincinnati
University College
Legal Assisting Program
Mail Location #207
Cincinnati, OH 45221

*University of Toledo
Legal Assisting Technology
Scott Park Campus
281 W. Bancroft Street
Toledo, OH 43606

OKLAHOMA

American Institute for
  Paralegal Studies, Inc.
530 N.W. 33rd Street
Oklahoma City, OK 73118

Northeastern State University
Paralegal Studies Program
Criminal Justice Department
Tahlequah, OK 74464

Oklahoma City University
Legal Assistant Program
2501 North Blackwelder
Box 128 B
Oklahoma City, OK 73106

*Oklahoma Junior College
  of Business & Technology
Paralegal/Legal Assistant
  Program
3232 Northwest 65
Oklahoma City, OK 73116

*Oklahoma Junior College of
  Business & Technology
Paralegal Department
7370 East 71st Street
Tulsa, OK 74133

Rogers State College
Will Rogers & College Hill
Claremore, OK 74017-2099

*Rose State College
Legal Assistant Program/Business Division
6420 Southeast 15th
Midwest City, OK 73110

Tri-County Area Vocational/
  Technical School
6101 Nowata Road
Bartlesville, OK 74006

*Tulsa Junior College
Business Service Division
909 South Boston Avenue
Tulsa, OK 74119

*University of Oklahoma
Paralegal Program, CLE Law
  Center
300 Timberdell, Rm. 314
Norman, OK 73019

OREGON

Bradford School
Legal Assisting Program
921 SW Washington
Portland, OR 97205

College of Legal Arts
Legal Assistant Studies Program
University Center Building
527 Southwest Hall,
  Suite 415
Portland, OR 97201

National Academy for
  Paralegal Studies, Inc.
Barclay Building, Suite 209
701 Main Street
Oregon City, OR 97045

Oregon State Department of
  Education
942 Lancaster Drive, N.E.
Salem, OR 97310

Portland Community College
Legal Assistant Program
Department of Government
  Services
12000 Southwest 49th Ave.
Portland, OR 97219

PENNSYLVANIA

Academy of Medical Arts &
  Business
Paralegal Programs
279 Boas Street
Harrisburg, PA 17102

Allegheny Community
  College
808 Ridge Avenue
Pittsburgh, PA 15212

American Institute for
  Paralegal Studies, Inc.
Pennsylvania Regional Office
LeMont Plaza
609 County Line Road
Huntingdon Valley, PA
  19006

Career Institute (The)
1825 JFK Boulevard
Philadelphia, PA 19103

*Cedar Crest College
Paralegal Studies Program
100 College Drive
Allentown, PA 18104-6169

*Central Pennsylvania Business
  School
Division of Legal Studies
College Hill Road
Summerdale, PA 17093-0309

Community College of
  Allegheny County
Boyce Campus
595 Beatty Road
Monroeville, PA 15146

*Duquesne University
Paralegal Program
711 Rockwell Hall
Pittsburgh, PA 15282

*Gannon University
Lawyer's Assistant Program
University Square
Erie, PA 16541

*Harrisburg Area Community
  College
Legal Assistant Program
3300 Cameron Street Road
Harrisburg, PA 17110

Indiana University of
  Pennsylvania
Paralegal Program
School of Business
Indiana, PA 15705

Katherine Gibbs School
Paralegal Program
Land Title Building
100 South Broad Street
Philadelphia, PA 19110

King's College
Legal Assistant Program
Department of Criminal
  Justice
Wilkes Barre, PA 18711

Maine Line Paralegal
  Institute
100 E. Lancaster
Wayne, PA 19087

Manor Junior College
Paralegal Studies Program
Fox Chase Road & Forest
  Avenue
Jenkintown, PA 19046-3399

*Marywood College
Legal Assistant Program
2300 Adams Avenue
Scranton, PA 18509

Northampton County Area
  Community College
Legal Assistant Cert.
  Program
3835 Green Pond Road
Bethlehem, PA 18017

*Peirce Junior College
Paralegal Studies Program
1420 Pine Street
Philadelphia, PA 19103

Penn State University
The Pittsburgh Center
337 Fourth Avenue
Pittsburgh, PA 15222

Penn State University
McKeesport Campus,
   Continuing Education
University Drive
McKeesport, PA 15132

Penn State University
Fayette Campus, Continuing
   Education
P.O. Box 519–Route 119N
Uniontown, PA 15401

Penn State University
Shenango Valley Campus,
   Continuing Education
147 Shenango Avenue
Sharon, PA 16146

Penn State University
Behrend College, Continuing
   Education
Station Road
Erie, PA 16563

Penn State University
State College Area, Continuing Education
109 Grange Building
University Park, PA 16802

Penn State University
Capital College, Continuing
   Education
Route 230
Middletown, PA 17057

Penn State University
Mont Alto Campus
Continuing Education
Mont Alto, PA 17237

Penn State University
York Campus, Continuing
   Education
1031 Edgecomb Avenue
York, PA 17403

Penn State University
Williamsport Area, Continuing Education
420 Broad Street
Montoursville, PA 17754

Penn State University
Hazleton Campus,
   Continuing Education
Highacres
Hazleton, PA 18201

Penn State University
Worthington Scranton
   Campus
120 Ridge View Drive
Dunmore, PA 18512

Penn State University
Wilkes-Barre Campus
Continuing Education
Lehman, PA 18627

Penn State University
Ogontz Campus, Continuing
  Education
1600 Woodland Road
Abington, PA 19001

Penn State University
Delaware Campus,
  Continuing Education
25 Yearsley Mill Road
Media, PA 19063

Penn State University
Berks Campus, Continuing
  Education
Tulpehocken Road, RD 5
P.O. Box 2150
Reading, PA 19608

Penn State University,
  Allentown
Continuing Education
Academic Building
Fogelsville, PA 18051

Pennsylvania State University
Continuing Education
610 Business Admn. Bldg.
University Park, PA 16802

Robert Morris College
Legal Assistant Cert. Program
Fifth Avenue at Sixth
Pittsburgh, PA 15219

St. Vincent College
Paralegal Certificate Program
Career Development Center
Latrobe, PA 15650-2690

*The Philadelphia Institute
1926 Arch Street
Philadelphia, PA 19103

University of Pittsburgh
Legal Studies Program
435 Cathedral of Learning
Pittsburgh, PA 15260

*Villanova University
Paralegal Program
Villanova, PA 19085

Western School of Health &
  Business Careers
Paralegal Specialist Program
Chamber of Commerce
411 Seventh Avenue
Pittsburgh, PA 15219

*Widener University
Institute for Professional
  Development
Room 135, Kapelski Center
Chester, PA 19013

PUERTO RICO

Universidad de Ponce
Legal Assistant Program
P.O. Box 648
Ponce, PR 00733

Universidad de Ponce
Legal Assistant Program
Avenida De Diego 700
Caparra Terrace, PR 00920

RHODE ISLAND

Johnson & Wales University
Office Careers Institute
8 Abbott Park Place
Providence, RI 02903

Roger Williams College
Paralegal Studies
Old Ferry Road
Bristol, RI 02809

Salve Regina-The Newport
College
Legal Assistant Program
Newport, RI 02840

SOUTH CAROLINA

Beaufort Technical College
Paralegal Program
P.O. Box 1288–Ribaut Road
Beaufort, SC 29902

Columbia Junior College
Professional Center for Paralegal Studies
829 Gervais Street
Columbia, SC 29201

*Greenville Technical College
Paralegal Department
P.O. Box 5616 Station B
Greenville, SC 29606-5616

Horry-Georgetown Tech.
College
Paralegal Program
P.O. Box 1966
Highway 501 E.
Conway, SC 29526

*Midlands Technical College
Post Offfice Box 2408
Columbia, SC 29202

National Academy for
Paralegal Studies, Inc.
P.O. Box 3588
Rock Hill, SC 29731

Trident Technical College
P.O. Box 10367
Charleston, SC 29411

Watterson College
Paralegal Studies Program
1064 Gardner Road
Suite 105
Charleston, SC 29407

SOUTH DAKOTA

National Academy for
Paralegal Studies, Inc.
226 N. Phillips Ave., #204
Sioux Falls, SD 57102

Yankton College
Legal Assistant Program
12th & Douglas
Yankton, SD 57078

TENNESSEE

Bristol College
2409 Volunteer Parkway
P.O. Box 4366
Bristol, TN 37625

*Cleveland State Community
College
Legal Assistant Program
P.O. Box 3570
Cleveland, TN 37320-3570

Edmondson Junior College
Legal Assistant Program
1166 Murpheesboro
Suite 200
Nashville, TN 37217

Edmondson Junior College
Paralegal Program
3635 Brainard Road
Chattanooga, TN 37411

Jackson State College
Office of Continuing
Education
P.O. Box 2467
Jackson, TN 38302-2467

Knoville Business College
Paralegal Program
720 North 5th Avenue
Knoxville, TN 37917

Memphis State University
Department of Business
Administration
Memphis, TN 38152

Milligan College
Legal Assistant Program
Milligan College, TN 37682

National Academy for
Paralegal Studies, Inc.
5100 Wheelis Drive, Ste. 100
Memphis, TN 38117

Pellissippi State Technical
Community College
10915 Hardin Valley Road
Knoxville, TN 37933-0900

*Southeastern Paralegal
Institute
2416 21st Avenue, South
Third Floor
Nashville, TN 37212

State Technical Institute
Legal Assistant Program
5983 Macon Cove
Memphis, TN 38134-7693

University of Tennessee
Paralegal Training Program
608 Stokely Management
   Center
Knoxville, TN 37996-0565

TEXAS

Career Institute
3015 Richmond Avenue
Houston, TX 77098

Collin County Community
   College District
Legal Assistant Program
2200 West University
McKinney, TX 75070

Del Mar College
Legal Assistant Program
Baldwin & Ayers
Corpus Christi, TX 78404

Durham Nixon-Clay Business
   College
119 West Eighth Street
P.O. Box 1626
Austin, TX 78767

East Texas State University
Dept. of Political Science
Commerce, TX 75428

El Centro College
Legal Assistant Program
Main and Lamar
Dallas, TX 75202

El Paso County Community
   College
Legal Assistant Program
P.O. Box 20500
El Paso, TX 79998

Executive Secretarial School
Legal Assistant/Paralegal
   Program
4849 Greenville Avenue
Suite 200
Dallas, TX 75206

Grayson County College
Legal Assistant Program
6101 Grayson Drive
Denison, TX 75020

Houston Community College
   System
Legal Assistant Program
4701 Dixon Street
Houston, TX 77007

Kilgore College
Legal Assisting Program
1100 Broadway
Kilgore, TX 75662

Lamar University
Continuing Education
P.O. Box 10008
Beaumont, TX 77710

*Lee College
Legal Assistant Program
511 South Whiting Street
Baytown, TX 77520-4703

North Harris County
  College
Legal Assistant Program
2700 W. W. Thorne,
  Suite W115
Houston, TX 77075

Odessa College
Legal Assistant Program
201 W. University
Odessa, TX 79764

San Antonio College
Legal Assistant Program
1300 San Pedro Avenue
San Antonio, TX 78284

*Southeastern Paralegal
  Institute
Legal Assistant Program
5440 Harvest Hill,
  Suite 200
Dallas, TX 75230

*Southern Methodist
  University
Legal Asst. Certificate
  Program
SMU Box 275
Dallas, TX 75275

Southwest Texas State
  University
Lawyer's Assistant Program
Evans Liberal Arts Building
San Marcos, TX 78666

*Southwestern Paralegal
  Institute
Basic Legal Assistant
  Studies
2211 Norfolk, Suite 420
Houston, TX 77098-4096

Tarrant County Jr. College
Northeast Campus
828 Harwood Road
Hurst, TX 76054

Texas Para-Legal School,
  Houston
608 Fannin, Suite 1903
Houston, TX 77002

Texas Woman's University
Dept. of History &
  Government
P.O. Box 23974
Denton, TX 76204

University of Houston at
   Clear Lake City
Legal Studies Program
2700 Bay Area Blvd.
Houston, TX 77058

University of Texas,
   Arlington
Paralegal Program
Dept. of Political Science
Arlington, TX 76019

University of Texas,
   Austin
Legal Assistant Program
P.O. Box 7879
Austin, TX 78713-7879

Video Technical Institute
   (VTI)
Institute for Paralegal Studies
2505 N. Highway 360,
   Suite 420
Grand Prairie, TX 75053

West Texas State University
Department of History and
   Political Science
Canyon, TX 79016

Woodland Paralegal Institute
5 Grogans Park, Suite 200
Woodland, TX 77381

UTAH

*Utah Valley Community
   College
Legal Assistant Program
1200 South 800 West
Orem, UT 84058

*Westminster College
Legal Assistant Cert. Program
1840 South 1300 East
Salt Lake City, UT 84105

VERMONT

Champlain College
Post Office Box 670
Burlington, VT 05402

Woodbury College
Paralegal Studies Program
659 Elm Street
Montpelier, VT 05602

VIRGINIA

American Institute for
   Paralegal Studies, Inc.
500 E. Main Street, Suite 628
Norfolk, VA 23514

Central Virginia Community
   College
3506 Wards Road
Lynchburg, VA 24502

Elizabeth Brant School
Staunton, VA 24401

Ferrum College
Legal Assistant Program
Ferrum, VA 24088

*J. Sargeant Reynolds
Community College
Parham Road Campus
P.O. Box C-32040
Richmond, VA 23261-2040

*James Madison University
Department of Political
Science
Paralegal Studies Program
Harrisonburg, VA 22807

*Marymount University
Paralegal Studies Program
2807 North Glebe Road
Arlington, VA 22207-4299

Mountain Empire Community
College
Legal Assistant Program
Drawer 700
Big Stone Gap, VA 24219

National Academy for
Paralegal Studies, Inc.
1022 Court Street
P.O. Box 1359
Lynchburg, VA 24505

National Institute of Paralegal
Training
Tyson's Corner Education
Center
1880 Howard Avenue
Vienna, VA 22311

*Northern Virginia Commu-
nity College
Legal Assisting Program
3001 N. Beauregard
Alexandria, VA 22311

Para-Legal Institute
7700 Leesburg Pike, Ste. 305
Falls Church, VA 22043

Thomas Nelson Community
College
Legal Assistant Program
P.O. Box 9407
Hampton, VA 23670

Tidewater Community
College
Legal Assistant Program
1700 College Crescent
Virginia Beach, VA 23456

University of Richmond
University College Evening
School
Richmond, VA 23173

*Virginia Intermont College
Paralegal Studies Program
Bristol, VA 24201

Virginia Western Community
College
3095 Colonial Avenue, S.W.
Roanoke, VA 24038

WASHINGTON

American Institute for
Paralegal Studies, Inc.
1700 Security Pacific Plaza
777 108th Avenue, N.E.
Bellevue, WA 98004

Bellevue Community College
3000 Landerholm Circle, S.E.
Bellevue, WA 98009-2037

Central Washington
University
Program in Law & Justice
Ellensburg, WA 98926

City University
Legal Studies Programs
16661 Northup Way
Bellevue, WA 98008

*Edmonds Community College
Legal Assistant Program
20000 68th Avenue West
Lynnwood, WA 98036

*Highline Community College
Legal Assistant Program
Community College District 9
Midway, WA 98031

Lower Columbia College
Legal Assistant Program
1600 Maple
Longview, WA 98632

Metropolitan Business College
2501 SE State Highway 160
Port Orchard, WA 98366

National Academy for
Paralegal Studies, Inc.
P.O. Box 21873
Seattle, WA 98111-3873

Pierce College
Paralegal Studies Program
9401 Farwest Drive SW
Tacoma, WA 98498

Spokane Community College
Legal Assistant Program
North 1810 Greene Street
Spokane, WA 99207

Univ. of Washington,
Extension
Paralegal Studies Program
5001 25th Avenue, NE
GH-21
Seattle, WA 98195

WEST VIRGINIA

Fairmont State College
Legal Assistant Program
Division of Social Science
Fairmont, WV 26554

*Marshall University
Community College
Legal Assistant Program
Huntington, WV 25701

National Academy for
Paralegal Studies, Inc.
100 Carmel Road
Wheeling, WV 26003

WISCONSIN

American Institute for Paralegal Studies, Inc.
710 N. Plakington, Ste. 500
Milwaukee, WI 53203

Carthage College
Paralegal Program
2001 Alford Drive
Kenosha, WI 53140-1994

*Chippewa Valley Tech.
College
Legal Assistant Program
620 W. Clairmont Avenue
Eau Claire, WI 54701

Concordia University,
Wisconsin
Paralegal Degree Program
12800 North Lake Shore
Drive
Mequon, WI 53092-9652

*Lakeshore Technical College
Legal Assistant Program
1290 North Avenue
Cleveland, WI 53105

*Milwaukee Area Technical
College
Legal Assistant Program
700 West State Street
Milwaukee, WI 53233

WYOMING

Casper College
Legal Assistant Program
125 College Drive
Casper, WY 82601

Laramie County Community
College
Legal Assistant Program
1400 E. College Drive
Cheyenne, WY 82007